Big Buicks

A Source Book

EDITED AND ANNOTATED BY
R. Perry Zavitz

Motorbooks International
Publishers & Wholesalers Inc
Osceola, Wisconsin 54020, USA

Bookman Publishing

Baltimore, Maryland

Printed in the U.S.A.
Copyright 1984 in U.S.A. by Bookman Dan!, Inc.

ISBN 0-934780-45-5

First Edition
First Printing

Inquiries may be directed to:
Bookman Publishing Division
Bookman Dan!, Inc.
P.O. Box 13492
Baltimore, Maryland 21203

Book trade distribution by:
Motorbooks International
P. O. Box 2
Osceola, Wisconsin 54020

Contents

*In 1934, Buick introduced
its Series 40 models. They were
designed to be smaller and less
expensive to compete with lower
priced cars. The example seen
here is the 5-passenger Club
Sedan, Model 41. It was built on
an "X" cross-member-design
frame (as were all Buicks from
1933 to 1959), and featured a
new knee-action front suspension,
which incorporated Delco-
Lovejoy shock absorbers and a
rear anti-sway bar.*

Preface

The muscle cars of the 1960s and 1970s trace their origin to the 1936 Buick Century. That was a new model which Buick made from the components of their other models. The Century combined a body scarcely larger than that of the Special (Buick's smallest) with the new and powerful 120 hp engine of the big Roadmaster and Limited series. There was a horsepower race underway in the 30s and early 40s. The Century was right up there with the rest, as it pioneered the use of compound carburetion.

Unfortunately, the Second World War interrupted all civilian car production. After the Allied victories, car production resumed, but without the Buick Century. There was such a pent-up demand for new cars after the war, that anything new would sell. When that demand was met, Buick revived the Century for 1954. It was essentially the same type of car that it had been before the war.

This was an appropriate time to re-introduce the Century. When the Buick Special got its new V-8, the Century reappeared, but not with the Special's engine. It used the already-proven, big V-8 of the large Super and Roadmaster series. Yet, this powerful motor was placed in the smaller, lighter Special body. The Century was a hybrid. More importantly, it was a factory hot-rod. The postwar Century's popularity was noticeably greater than before the war.

The public was dreaming of fast, good-looking cars in the postwar age, and the Century was that dream come true and affordable for thousands of buyers. With increasing affluence in the postwar society, many more people could have a new Buick of their very own. That helped catapult it ahead of Plymouth in sales.

Surely, it is more than coincidence that Buick's spectacular rise in popularity occurred when the Century was being marketed. During those years, Buick rose from sixth place to third in sales.

But, what goes up must come down, even in car popularity. When the economic recession of 1958 hurt car sales, Buick was hit hard. A revolution took place in its 1959 line-up. Along with totally new styling, there was a totally new set of model names. In the middle was Invicta, but it continued the Century formula of the bigger engine in the smaller body.

Now, Invicta is not the most inspiring and exciting name Buick could have chosen. That matter was resolved gradually during the 1962 and 1963 model years, however, as the Wildcat took over the top performance function for Buick.

During the heyday of the muscle cars, Buick did not forget the performance-minded buyers who wanted plush, full-size passenger cars—cars which could easily keep up with all the others in the fast lane. The Wildcat did that job quite admirably.

By the end of the 1960s, however, two things were working against high performance cars. Insurance rates for high-powered cars were raised to discouraging levels. Also, concern in Washington about air pollution from car exhausts led to legislation requiring pollution reducing engine equipment and design. Unfortunately, these pollution controls had serious side effects which ran counter to good performance.

In an attempt to spark renewed interest in the high-performance full-size passenger cars, Buick introduced the Centurion for 1971. It perpetuated the Century/Invicta/Wildcat tradition of big, powerful engines in relatively smaller full-size bodies. Though performance was maintained, despite increasingly restrictive regulations regarding exhaust emissions, the public had lost much of its interest in high-performance.

When the 1973 production run ended, Buick dropped the Centurion and offered nothing to replace it. At that time, when the Arab oil embargo was suddenly felt, it was totally inappropriate to have a big, tire-screaming car. An exciting era had come to a close.

Since 1936, Buick had showed the world the easy way to build affordable, full-size, high-performance passenger cars. Some competitors followed Buick's lead in this area, but few, if any, enjoyed quite the success that Buick did.

London, Ontario
June, 1984

There were several new features that the 1936 Buick introduced. For the first time, model names were used at Buick, along with the series designation. The Series 60 was also called Century. There had been a Series 60 Buick since the 1930 model. It was a six-cylinder car in its initial year. Thereafter, the Series 60 was powered by a straight-eight engine. It may not have been Buick's smallest eight in each model year, but neither was it the largest. Not until the 1936 model, that is.

A new eight-cylinder engine was introduced in the 1936 models for the big Roadmaster and Limited Buicks. (As had been Buick's constant practice, it had overhead valves.) Someone got the bright idea of putting this engine in the smaller body of the Special. That would give the lighter car considerably better performance. The new engine weighed only 843 lbs, compared to 1,008 of the engine it replaced. So, the new 320.2 cubic inch 120 hp engine was shoehorned under the hood of the Special. Actually, some body modifications were made, because the wheelbase was 122 inches, 4 more than the Special.

This blend of the best of both—smaller body but larger engine—was called the Century. The car lived up to its name. It was soon discovered that the speedometer needle could top 100 mph, phenomenal in the thirties. It had 27 more horsepower than the Special, but weighed only 120 lbs more.

At $1,095, it cost only $210 more than the Special. That was a bargain. Only Cadillac, Imperial, Lincoln K, Packard, Pierce-Arrow, supercharged Auburn, and Duesenberg had more power than the Century. Needless to say, all those cars were considerably more costly.

In its first model year, 25,980 Centurys were produced. That may seem low, but not when viewed in the proper context. It must be recognized that this was a new kind of car. A high-performance car available at a relatively low price was not something most people were looking for. Car buyers had to be conditioned to that idea. It would take time, especially in the post-depression recovery days.

Buick was not about to give up. With 15.4% of their production devoted to the new Century, it was continued in the restyled 1937 body. And, as before, it was available in a whole range of body types, from four-door sedans to sport coupes, and convertibles to chassis only.

The engine now produced 130 hp. Obviously there were some buyers interested in low-cost performance cars. Production was up more than 9,000 to 35,093, and accounted for 15.9% of the year's Buicks.

The next year, however, was not so good. The Century's engine (still shared with Roadmaster and Limited) was raised to 141 hp. Only the 12 and 16-cylinder cars and Pierce-Arrow Eight developed greater power. Yet, production of the 1938 Century fell 45% to only 19,287. And its share of the Buick production pie dropped to 11.4%. So, generous horsepower was a strong selling point with a limited number of buyers at this time.

For 1939, Century production grew over 26.5%, but its share of Buick's total output was steady at 11.7%. The engine remained at 141 hp, but as some of the other high-powered cars were dropping by the wayside, the Century's powerful engine was becoming a bit more obvious. Evidently, only a few people saw the benefits, though.

Production retreated again. For the 1940 models, it dropped to 18,775, but the Century only accounted for 66 out of every 1,000 Buicks that year. A further Century reduction in total number of Buicks built occurred for 1941, to just 5.5%, but it was a bigger year, so the actual number of Centurys rose to 20,907.

Nineteen forty-two was a short year. Because of the war, production of civilian cars was halted in February. Although the Century was still made, the total was a mere 4,551. And those were only two-door sedanets and 4-door sedans. All other body types were discontinued.

The 1941 and 1942 Centurys were technically the most interesting. Sharing, as usual, the Roadmaster/Limited engine, Century featured "compound carburetion." It was probably the earliest production example of multiple carburetors. With two 2-barrel carburetors, the engine developed 165 hp. That was the highest in the industry at the time, equalled only by the biggest 1942 Packards.

Buick literature was fairly consistent in this era, with a large catalogue and a cheap folder (based on the same art) for each year. The major exceptions were 1940 and 1941 when the huge Limited models were not covered in the large catalogues (although they appeared in the cheap folders), but had positively huge Limited catalogues of their own. The Limited was back for 1942, although for the last time, but was covered in the main catalogue. The sizes of the catalogues varied widely, but the folders were nearly always 8½x11, two-fold items. Factory photos of 1937, 1939 and 1942 Buicks appear opposite. A 1936 Buick "high performance" ad appears on the following pages. An exerpt from the 1978 catalogue appears on page 4.

HOT? IT'S

Styled to the latest tasteful minute! Here is a mature development of modern design that turns streamlining into dreamlining

234

A BALL OF FIRE!

That's what 5,000 dealers and salesmen said when they pre-viewed the new Buick line-up for 1936!

DAY by day they rolled into Flint by the trainload — veteran Buick dealers who had heard advance rumors that something big was in the air—something spectacular was about to break, in the four stellar Buick series for 1936.

And when they examined that brilliant array—the complete line of cars—the Buick Series 40 Special, the Buick Series 60 Century, the Buick Series 80 Roadmaster, the Buick Series 90 Limited—when they heard the sales program and the engineering report — when they saw the advertising and sales promotion program—you should have seen and heard them rise up and cheer.

There's no doubt about it—Buick is the news—Buick is the sensation—Buick is the Buy for 1936!

An opportunity to "go to town"

By this time you've seen the eye-filling beauty and year ahead style of these new Buicks.

But here's something you can't find out till you get behind the wheel.

Every car in the line will step from 10 to 60 m.p.h. in 21.4 seconds or less. The figures for each series of cars run—20.7—19.6—20.7 and 21.4.

The biggest car in the line handles with small car ease—and the lowest-priced car has big-car comfort and roominess.

We threw away all the old dimensions of size and performance — kept only the Buick fundamentals of dependability — the great-powered valve-in-head straight eight engine, the torque tube drive, the sealed chassis, and honest engineering—and set out to build a line of cars that would startle the world.

What the public wants—*these cars have in generous measure.* Solid steel "Turret Top" Body by Fisher—Knee-Action — Buick improved Hydraulic Brakes — and Anolite Pistons, which literally wear like iron, weigh half as much, and increase bearing life 150%.

That's why the unanimous verdict of those 5,000 dealers and salesmen who viewed the whole program was, "Hot? It's a ball of fire!"

Or as one big east coast operator put it —"Ride 'em and reap!"

There's 93 horsepower in the Buick Special—120 horsepower in the other three series — and with it, the easy accessibility and gasoline economy of the famous valve-in-head straight eight as Buick builds it

Anolite! *That's the name of these new Buick pistons that wear like iron and increase connecting rod bearing life 150%*

Ride 'em and reap! *When a prospect gets behind this wheel, the sale is as good as made. Also notice that stunning instrument panel*

Buick 8

FIRST OF THE GENERAL MOTORS CARS

NOVEMBER 1935

PRICES?

$765 AND UP

list for the new Buicks at Flint and subject to change without notice. Standard and special accessory groups on all models at extra cost. All Buick prices include safety glass throughout as standard equipment. Convenient GMAC time payment plan

Room to let! *Even the trunks are increased in size—and when it comes to inside capacity, the line includes six and eight passenger models*

235

1954-1956

The Century was a war casualty. It did not come back at the end of World War II. Not right away, that is. After the auto industry finally got caught up in the backlog of orders from three-and-a-half years of no production, and the ability of more people to buy new cars in the postwar years, Buick revived its Century. It was felt the time had come when this hot-rod would appeal to more buyers. Performance was on the minds of more people now.

The postwar model followed its earlier tradition—combining the Special body and the Roadmaster motor. The Special got a new V-8 for 1954, but the Century did not use it. Instead, it was fitted with the Roadmaster's 322 cubic inch V-8, which had been introduced the year before. The 1954 edition developed 200 hp. For the dwindling group of buyers insisting on a manual transmission, engine output was 195 hp. In a car just 70 lbs heavier than the Special, outstanding performance was inevitable with either engine.

The revived Series 60 Century, with Tom McCahill's foot on the accelerator, got to 60 mph from a standing start in 11.8 seconds. His test car had Dynaflow transmission, and he got the best time by starting in low and shifting to drive. He reached a maximum speed of 110 mph. Yet this hot car as a four-door sedan had a base price of just $2,520. That was competitive with the top end of the Chevrolet or Ford price range.

Century came in a full-line of body types like a four-door sedan, two-door Riviera hardtop, convertible, and even a four-door all-steel station wagon. For those interested in getting a lot of groceries home in a hurry, the Century Estate Wagon was the answer, but only 1,563 were made. The most popular was the Riviera hardtop, of which Buick built 45,710.

Hardtops were hot sellers at this time. Buick pioneered this body style in 1949, and was promoting them as vigorously as anyone. Called Riviera in any Buick series, it accounted for nearly 56% of the 81,982 Centurys built for 1954.

It seems that no exclusive sales literature for this dazzling performer was published. Century was included in the regular full-line catalogue. But surprisingly, a description of the convertible was conspicuously absent, though 2,790 were made. In addition to the catalogue, magazine advertisements let everyone know about "the return of the Century," still without promoting the convertible.

The success of the first postwar Century assured its return for 1955. Production for its second year nearly doubled the first. The 158,798 Centurys built for 1955 were substantially more than those made in any of the seven model years of prewar Buick Century production.

The horsepower race was going full bore, with Buick in the thick of it. Its 322 cubic inch displacement V-8 was given increased compression to improve output. The 9:1 compression, up from 8.5:1 the year before, resulted in an 18% increase to 236 hp, with or without Dynaflow. That, in virtually the same Special body of the previous model, made the 1956 Century truly a high performance car.

"Motor Trend's" test of the Century with Dynaflow yielded a 0 to 60 time of 9.8 seconds, and a top speed of 106.5 mph. They also tested a Roadmaster, for comparison. It needed 13.8 second in the 0 to 60 run, and had a top speed of 104.1. Little wonder

"Science and Mechanics" magazine described the Century as "sort of a hotrod dressed in mink."

A new choice for Century buyers was the mid-year introduction of a second Riviera, a four-door hardtop. Despite its late appearance, this new Riviera became the Century's second best selling body type, with 55,088 made. The two-door Riviera remained as the top seller. Its production reached a total of 80,338. One of the rarest 1956 Centurys was the convertible, but with 5,588 made, it was not really rare for a ragtop.

Price hikes seemed inevitable, but for the Century they were quite modest, being in the neighborhood of $28 to $67. The Estate Wagon was actually reduced by $295 to $3,175. Other body types ranged from about $2,500 for the rare two-door sedan (only 270 produced) to $2,991 for the convertible.

No exclusive Century sales brochures were issued for 1955, but that was not unusual. The other Buick series were given the same treatment. All series were covered in the sales catalogues. A folder appeared in the spring of 1955 to promote the four-door Rivieras in all four Buick model lines.

The usual changes marked the 1956 Century. As surely as a grille redesign, there was also the increase in engine power. The compression of the 322 cubic inch V-8 was jacked up to 9.5:1, and the advertised brake horsepower was raised to 255. This was, however, to be the last year for the 322 engine under the Century hood.

Its performance, according to Tom McCahill, was "as hot as the mustache of a cross-eyed flame eater." By starting in low with the Variable Pitch Dynaflow, which was now standard, and shifting up, he got a 0 to 60 time of just 9.8 seconds. Top speed was in the area of 120 mph. Elsewhere, the elapsed time for a quarter mile acceleration took 17.1 seconds. At least as far as the Century's performance was concerned, the slogan was right. This was the "Best Buick Yet."

Some interesting changes to body types were made for the 1956 Century. The rare two-door sedan was deleted. Records show that just one four-door sedan was made, so it was effectively deleted as well. Buick was emphasizing hardtops. The four-door Riviera was offered in two versions—standard and Deluxe. They were given the designation 63 and 630, respectively. The Deluxe edition outsold the regular by about a 7 to 5 ratio.

The price premium for the Deluxe four-door Riviera over the standard was just $16. Prices for each of the 1956 Centurys was $2,963 for the two-door Riviera; $3,025, four-door Riviera; $3,041, four-door Deluxe Riviera; $3,306, convertible; and, $3,256, Estate Wagon. On the surface, these prices appear to be up substantially from 1955, however, Dynaflow was now included in the base price.

Tradition remained with the Century being described along with the other Buick series in the regular sales brochures. It was frequently featured in magazine ads, as well.

The 1954-1956 Buick literature program included similar large and small full-line catalogues for each year. Century excerpts are included here for 1954 (see pages 12-15), 1955 (see page 16)) and 1956 (see page 17). A fascinating example of the perceived performance potential of these cars is the Offenhauser "Buick Power," folder issued in 1956 (see pages 18-20). A 1954 Special factory photo appears opposite.

Buick CENTURY

Back again – Dazzling Performer in Scintilla

CENTURY 2-Door 6-Passenger RIVIERA, Model 66R, 122-in. Wheelbase, 200 Horsepower with Dynaflow

TO YOU who recall the Buick CENTURY of prewar years, little more need be said than that this spectacular performer is now back in the line—in modern power and performance and new-day dress.

To you who never knew its prowess—these simple facts will explain the news excitement of the return of the CENTURY:

This is the Buick—reborn in 1954—that has top-of-the-line power in the extra-compact chassis of 122-inches.

Thus, it has the most favorable power-to-weight ratio in Buick history—and the dazzling performance that results from this ratio.

But beyond its 200-horsepower Fireball V8 engine and its highly maneuverable chassis—beyond the beauty of its stunning new body and the rich comfort of its interiors, its visibility, its handling, its ride—the big news of this big-performance automobile is *price*. For the CENTURY returns in 1954 at a price level just a step above Buick's lowest.

ting Dress...

Swing-Away Doors and Tilt-Away Front Seats
insure far more ease in entering and leaving
the spacious interior of the 1954 CENTURY
Riviera. Note the reverse-slant front
pillars that permit an extra-wide sweep
in the panoramic windshield.

Pretty Soft for Performance Lovers is the comfort of the dazzling CENTURY Sedan's interior. Here, rich Nylon fabrics over buoyant foam-rubber seat cushions put color and comfort on a par with the performance of the CENTURY.

1954 Buick CENTURY

WITH THE spectacular performance of the CENTURY, as it is reborn in 1954, goes a long list of the engineering advances brought forth in this pace-setting Buick year.

There is the long, low styling—with the body line lowered a full three inches, yet maintaining full road clearance.

There is the superb visibility and grace of greater glass area—and the comfort of seeing the high-line front fenders through the swept-back panoramic windshield.

There is the responsive handling of even lower over-all steering-gear ratios—plus, at your option, the convenience of Buick Safety

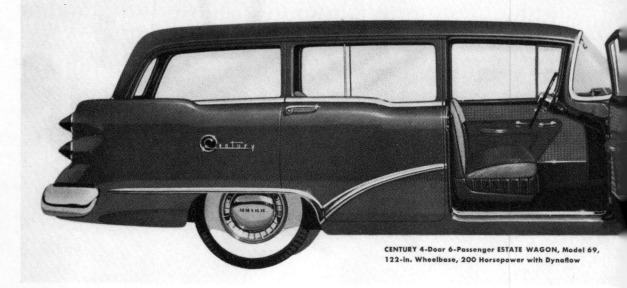

CENTURY 4-Door 6-Passenger ESTATE WAGON, Model 69, 122-in. Wheelbase, 200 Horsepower with Dynaflow

CENTURY 4-Door 6-Passenger SEDAN, Model 61,
122-in. Wheelbase, 200 Horsepower with Dynaflow

Power Steering and Power Brakes.

And, of course, there is the ruggedness of Buick's construction—of an X-braced frame, 122-inch wheelbase, torque-tube drive, coil-spring cushioning, wide Safety-Ride rims mounting soft, low-pressure tires that are now quieter underway.

CENTURY 2-Door 6-Passenger CONVERTIBLE, Model 66C,
122-in. Wheelbase, 200 Horsepower with Dynaflow

Front-Page News In More Ways Than One Is The All-Steel Buick Estate Wagon—for this famed Buick body style now comes in its *first* all-steel version—in a new, lower price range—and with the sheer brilliance of CENTURY performance.

In this tremendously able traveler, you get versatility with verve. You get the correct car for casual country living *and* the correct car for dress affairs. You get stretch-out room for six, plus abundant loading room. And you get this luxury-fitted, dual-purpose, all-steel beauty at a *budget* price.

Century 4-Door 6-Passenger Sedan, Model 61, 122-in. Wheelbase, 236 Horsepower.

1955 BUICK CENTURY *Spectacular Performance at Modest Price*

Century 2-Door 6-Passenger Riviera, Model 66R, 122-in. Wheelbase, 236 Horsepower.

Century 2-Door 6-Passenger Convertible, Model 66C, 122-in. Wheelbase, 236 Horsepower.

1956 BUICK CENTURY
for the performance-minded...
America's biggest
horsepower-per-dollar buy

CENTURY 6-Passenger, 4-Door RIVIERA, Model 63, 122-inch wheelbase, 255 horsepower

CENTURY 6-Passenger, 2-Door RIVIERA,
Model 66R, 122-inch wheelbase, 255 horsepower

CENTURY 6-Passenger, 2-Door CONVERTIBLE, Model 66, 122-inch wheelbase, 255 horsepower

THE PERFECT COMBINATION

The Offenhauser "Eldorado" Type Dual Quad Manifoid

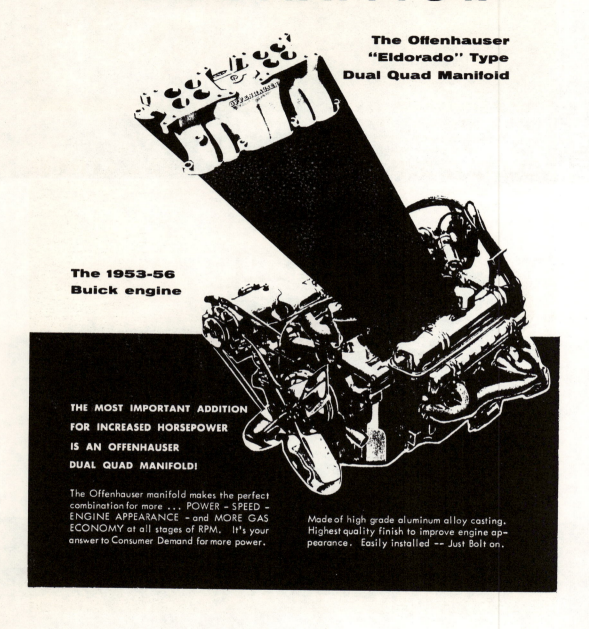

The 1953-56 Buick engine

THE MOST IMPORTANT ADDITION
FOR INCREASED HORSEPOWER
IS AN OFFENHAUSER
DUAL QUAD MANIFOLD!

The Offenhauser manifold makes the perfect combination for more ... POWER - SPEED - ENGINE APPEARANCE - and MORE GAS ECONOMY at all stages of RPM. It's your answer to Consumer Demand for more power.

Made of high grade aluminum alloy casting. Highest quality finish to improve engine appearance. Easily installed -- Just Bolt on.

power is necessary

Every year, gains in New Car Horsepower Ratings indicate the power trend. Offenhauser Power Equipment is the key to . . .

BIGGER SALES VOLUME

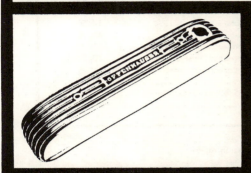

OFFENHAUSER VALVE COVERS
FOR ALL BUICK V8 ENGINES

Heavy top grade aluminum alloy castings, highly polished for engine beauty. Finned top permits faster heat dissipation, reduces valve tappet noise. It's an addition to give your customer that extra feeling of pride in his new Buick. For that distinctive, custom built, sports car look, install Offenhauser valve covers.

During the next few months this beautiful Buick Century Estate Wagon will be touring the major cities of the United States. It's completely equipped with Offenhauser power products.

WATCH FOR IT.

MORE SALES---PROFITS

Dealership acceptance of our power products has been terrific. Thousands of authorized automobile dealers are now profitably selling and installing our manifolds, valve covers, air cleaners and other power accessories.

HOW ABOUT YOU?

more air --- less gas?

A question that arises most often is "If I install a dual carburetor manifold, will I use more fuel?" The answer is "No." You will use more air and less fuel. Dual-quad or Dual-triple manifolds equalize fuel distribution to all cylinders, resulting in the perfect combination for power, economy and performance.

Used with the Buick Factory kits now available *, Offenhauser manifolds put the Buick horsepower rating in a class with the top competition stock cars. In short, it makes it one of the hottest cars in America.

Part No.	Description	List
3412	Dual-quad manifold satin finish	$89.50
3412	Dual-quad manifold Polished	99.95
3413	Combination dual-triple manifold less kit - Satin finish	75.00
3413	Combination dual-triple manifold less kit - Polished	85.45
3414	Manifold kit for 4-bolt carburetors	14.50
3415	Manifold kit for 3-bolt carburetors	14.50
3416	Valve Covers	43.50
3417	Quad mesh type chromed air cleaner (not oil bath)	13.95
3418	Quad bonnet type chromed air cleaner (not oil bath)	13.95
3419	Chromed air cleaner 2-5/8" for carburetors used on dual-triple manifolds	3.95
3420	Chromed oil bath air cleaner 2-5/8" for carburetors used on dual-triple manifolds	9.95

* #1392654 – Camshaft, solid lifters, etc.
#1392626 – Special pistons for 10-1 compression ratio.

When you buy Automotive Power Products, remember ... the recognized name for peak performance in automotive power equipment is Offenhauser. In every Offenhauser unit, the highest standard of quality is rigidly maintained at all times.

DON'T TAKE CHANCES WITH OFF BRANDS!
When you install Offenhauser power equipment in your car, you're installing the finest that money can buy!

Offenhauser EQUIPMENT CORP.
5156 ALHAMBRA AVE., LOS ANGELES 32, CALIF.

An all new body and a bigger engine were features of the 1957 Century. The new chassis allowed a lower silhouette. The Century remained in its traditional format—a Special with the Roadmaster/Super engine.

The engine was enlarged in both bore and stroke. They were increased by just 1/8th and 1/5th of an inch, respectively. That yielded a displacement of 364 cubic inches—practically the same size as Cadillac. Again, compression was increased, topping 10.0:1. The result was an even 300 hp.

Despite the increased power, the new bodies were somewhat heavier. So, 0 to 60 now took 10.1 seconds. The Century was still a hot car for the money, even though performance was down and prices were up.

Prices ranged from $3,234 to $3,706. The four-door sedan was back, but the Deluxe four-door Riviera was gone. Noteworthy was the new Estate Wagon, also called the Caballero. During the redesign of the body, Century's Estate Wagon emerged as a hardtop. Not too often has the pillarless design been applied to station wagon bodies. There were 10,186 Caballeros produced, making it the most popular Buick wagon model of the year, in fact, one of the most popular Buick wagons of all time.

Leading the 1957 Century popularity list was the four-door Riviera hardtop. There were 26,589 of these made. Although there were only 4,085 convertibles produced, the rarest 1957 Century was the two-door sedan. Somehow just two of them managed to get assembled.

The literature situation continued in much the same manner as it had been. Century was included in the main catalogue along with the other series, and it appeared in a number of full-page magazine ads.

It was a very poor year for new car sales in 1958, and Buick took a particular beating in the market place. There were only superficial changes made to the Century's exterior, and they were hardly for the better. Chrome was applied like it was going out of style, and, to a degree, it was.

Weight of the 1958 was up 75-100 lbs, or more. That did not help performance, and there was no increase in horsepower for the first time with the V-8. The engine was stuck at 300 hp, though that was certainly not an embarrassment. The Century was still capable of getting to 60 mph from 0 in 10 seconds, and had a top speed of 110 mph. On the other hand, stopping was improved with new radial finned, air-cooled, aluminum front brakes.

Although not a popular item, air-suspension was on the Century option list. Prices for the various models rose about $100 to a range from $3,316 to $3,831. The same six body types were offered as in the previous year, including the two-door sedan. Again, only two were built. The four-door Riviera was the top selling Century model, but a relatively small number were made—just 15,171. The convertible (except for the two-door sedan) was the rarest model at 2,588 units. Caballero Estate Wagon production was down more than 56% to 4,456.

In fact, total Century production for the 1958 model year was a small 37,568, or only 57% of the much reduced 1957 model year total. Even though more Centurys were produced for 1958 than for any prewar year, it was disappointing for the booming postwar era. This was the last year for the Buick Century in this form. (The name was revived in the 1970s. See Buick Gran Sports Source Book.)

The advertising people at Buick, who probably foresaw a bad year ahead, tried hard to sell the 1958 Buick. The catalogue was large. Four-and-a-half of its 36 pages described and depicted the Century. Magazine ads also promoted the Century in particular—the last of the standard size Centurys.

Literature excerpts included here include the Century spread from the 1957 and 1958 full-line folders (see pages 22 and 23, respectively).

CENTURY

CENTURY 6-Passenger 2-Door RIVIERA, Model 66R, 122-inch Wheelbase, 300 Horsepower

CENTURY 6-Passenger 4-Door RIVIERA, Model 63, 122-inch Wheelbase, 300 Horsepower
Similar to the above in room, ride, power—and even more modestly priced—there's the stunning Century 4-Door Sedan, Model 61 (not illustrated).

CENTURY 6-Passenger 2-Door CONVERTIBLE, Model 66C, 122-inch Wheelbase, 300 Horsepower

CENTURY 6-Passenger 4-Door CABALLERO ESTATE WAGON, Model 69, 122-inch Wheelbase, 300 Horsepower

BUICK *Century* FOR '58

CENTURY 2-Door 6-Passenger CONVERTIBLE,
Model 66C, 122-in. Wheelbase, 300 Horsepower

CENTURY 4-Door 6-Passenger RIVIERA,
Model 63, 122-in. Wheelbase, 300 Horsepower

CENTURY 2-Door 6-Passenger RIVIERA,
Model 66R, 122-in. Wheelbase, 300 Horsepower

CENTURY 4-Door 6-Passenger SEDAN,
Model 61, 122-in. Wheelbase, 300 Horsepower

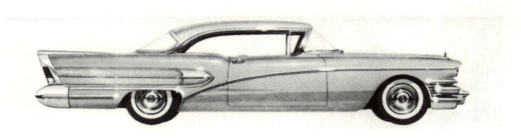

Invicta four-door sedan in
Magic-Mirror Wedgewood Blue

Invicta four-door hardtop in
Magic-Mirror Sierra Spruce

Invicta Estate Wagon in
Magic-Mirror Shalimar Blue

Invicta convertible in
Magic-Mirror Arctic White

Buick entered 1959 with many changes. Not only was there an entirely new body, but a total revision of model lines. All the previous series names were scrapped. Four new lines were introduced: LeSabre, Invicta, Electra, and Electra 225. If there had been a Century, it would have been the Invicta, because it continued the Century tradition of using Buick's bigger engine in its smaller body. In this case, Invicta was a LeSabre with the Electra engine.

And the Electra engine was not exactly a carry-over of the one used in the late Roadmaster. Bore and stroke had been increased to give a displacement of 401 cubic inches—General Motors' largest for the year. Compression was raised another half notch to 10.5:1. Horsepower was rated at 325, which equalled Cadillac (except Eldorado).

This powerplant was shoved into the new LeSabre body, which was only about 100 lbs heavier than the last Century. Performance minded Tom McCahill wound the Invicta up to 60 in 9.5 seconds, and let it go to 122 mph. The front fender portholes, the chrome spearsweep, and the Century name were all lost in the change to the 1959 models, but Buick performance continued.

The Invicta offered five body types, just as the Century before it: four-door sedan; two-door hardtop (the Riviera name was no longer used, so the two-door hardtop was called Sport Coupe); four-door hardtop; and the Estate Wagon, which dropped hardtop styling. The Invicta won "Motor Trend's" awards for "Best Styling" and "Best-Looking Wagon."

Prices rose only $10 on the Estate Wagon to $79 for the two hardtops. Invicta's prices ranged from $3,357 for the sedan to $3,841 for the wagon. Its most popular model was the four-door hardtop, 20,156 made, and the rarest was the Estate Wagon. With 5,231 wagons built, that production was 216 cars less than the convertible total. Altogether, 52,851 Invictas were built for 1959. That was up more than 40% from the previous year's Century production. At 18.5%, the first Invicta/Century took the largest share of Buick's production since 1956.

Literature and ads in the print media were much the same for the Invicta as they had been for the Century. There was an Invicta mailer which summarized favorable comments found in various car and industry magazines.

Some facelifting was done on the Invicta for its 1960 edition, but there was little change mechanically. The same 401 cubic inch engine was used. Although compression was reduced slightly to 10.25:1, advertised horsepower remained at 325. There was a minor reduction in weight, but hardly enough to enhance the car's already good performance.

An Invicta was subjected to an astounding endurance test in 1960. Buick could not publicize it, though, due to the Automobile Manufacturers Association moratorium on racing. A stock Invicta sedan was driven continually for 10,000 miles on the Daytona Speedway. A system was devised for a similar Invicta to inject fuel into the test car's tank at nearly top speed. Very brief stops were made every four hours to change drivers and check tires. When the run ended, after three-and-a-half days (5,000 minutes), the Invicta had set a record average speed of 120.186 mph.

A new model was added to the Invicta line-up for 1960. A three-seat Estate Wagon was now available. Previous Estate Wagons were only six-passenger models, so this was the first eight-passenger Buick wagon. The two-seat Estate Wagon continued, and remained at the same price as before, as did all the other Invicta models. The three-seat Estate Wagon was $3,841.

It was also the rarest of the 1960 Invictas. Just 1,605 were built, while 5,331 of the two-seat variety were made. The four-door hardtop was the most popular Invicta. Production totaled 35,999. In all, there were 45,411 1960 model Invictas produced. That was down about 14% from its first year.

For this year only, there were two Buick portfolios, one large and one small. Each included six color folders. There was one folder for each line (Electra and Electra 225 combined), and one folder each for the convertibles, Estate Wagons, and the engineering features of all lines. In addition, there was a long folding postcard type item for each of the three main series. There was also a full-line folder.

Literature excerpted for this chapter includes the 1959 (see pages 24, 26-27) and 1960 (see pages 28-29) full-line folders, as well as the 1960 "Buick Magazine" announcement issue (see pages 30-32).

INVICTA
THE MOST SPIRITED BUICK

Invicta two-door hardtop in Magic-Mirror Glacier Green

1960 Buick Invicta 4-Door Sedan in

1960 Buick Invicta 2-Door Hardtop in Magic-Mirror Titian Red

INVICTA SERIES

Magic-Mirror Lucerne Green

1960 Buick Invicta 4-Door Hardtop in Magic-Mirror Tahiti Beige and Cordovan

By **JIM WHIPPLE**
Technical Director, Car Life Magazine

BUICK'S NEW ENGINE-TRANSMISSION POWER TEAM IS TREMENDOUS

AFTER test driving the 1960 Buick I've come to the conclusion that it has as smooth acting an engine-transmission power team as any car in the business.

I drove a '60 Electra with 401-cubic inch V8 and Turbine Drive Transmission. Starting out in thick city traffic, I immediately rediscovered the unique advantage of Turbine Drive . . . the

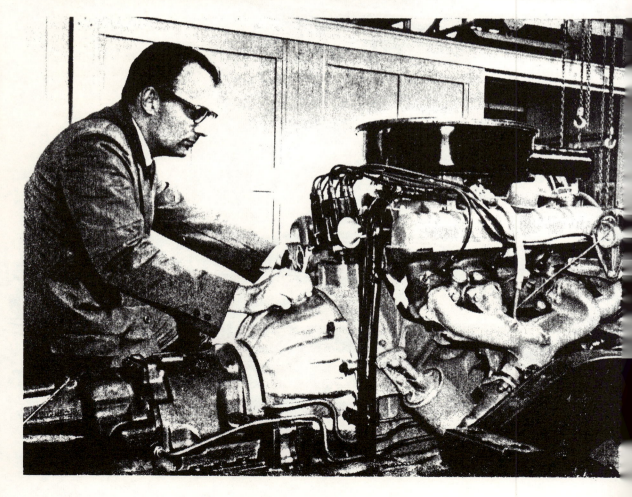

smooth response that only a geared torque converter can give.

Here's how it goes about its job: You may be rolling along at five to ten miles an hour when a traffic light turns green or a hole opens up and you want to get up to 30 or 35 miles per hour in a hurry.

Even some of the best automatics will put you through a downchange to a lower gear or take you through a noticeable surge and slackening off of acceleration through an upshift.

Other transmissions will give you a compromise low gear that provides a bit too much reduction and sends you zooming to the speed you want, then thumps into an upshift when you slack off the accelerator which rolls the car above the speed you wanted and you find yourself nudging the brake pedal.

Not so with the Turbine Drive '60 Buick. You get a direct and constant reaction between the amount of pressure you put on the accelerator pedal and the acceleration of the car itself. It's as smooth as Grandma's old Baker electric. After a mile or so, I found that I could put the Buick exactly where I wanted it at the correct speed as easily and smoothly as pouring syrup on a waffle. Turbine Drive comes closer to making heavy traffic pleasant than any transmission I know of.

But, smooth as it may be, the refined Turbine Drive Transmission on the '60 Buick is no lazy, sluggish "mush box." When you're passing smoothly and easily on a two-lane road and suddenly a car swings out of a hidden driveway to face you in the left lane a few hundred feet ahead . . . you don't have to hit the panic button, just squeeze the accelerator right down to the floor and "switch the pitch."

There's no neck-snapping downshift and jarring blast of noise that makes your passengers brace their feet and grab for the door handles . . . just a smooth surge like a rising wave, and almost instantly you're doing 60 or so and are back in line. It's hard to believe, but the stop watch proves that a Buick

will accelerate from 40 to 70 just as quickly as cars of equivalent weight and power with automatic transmissions that actually shift gears.

As Buick Transmission Engineer Harold Fischer explained it, "When you 'kickdown' for maximum acceleration on Turbine Drive you don't shift gears, you shift a constantly flowing stream of oil. There are no bands or clutches to release or engage, therefore nothing to wear out or lose correct adjustment."

I've talked about the Turbine Drive on the 1960 Buick first because it, rather than the engine, provides the special characteristics of drive smoothness that separates Buick from most other cars.

There are two versions of Buick's basic V8 in 1960, as last year, the 364-cubic inch V8 which powers the LeSabre, and the 401-inch engine standard on the Electra.

Although there have been numerous improvements through the basic engine, the horsepower and torque output remain the same. However, very few owners will feel need for more power.

E. H. Holtzkemper, Buick engineer, who briefed me on the new engines, pointed out a new engine option on the LeSabre. This is a 9.0 to 1 compression ratio engine available with Turbine Drive. Standard Turbine Drive engine on the LeSabre has a compression ratio of 10.25 to 1. The optional ratio lets you have your cake and eat it, too — Turbine Drive plus "regular" — 93 Octane gasoline, with several cents a gallon saving.

"However," said Mr. Holtzkemper, "the optional engine doesn't have all the advantages by any means. With 10.25 to 1 compression we get higher efficiency—more power per gallon and therefore more miles. So, even if the premium gasoline costs a few cents more, you'll need less of it.

"Engine efficiency and fuel economy is up on all models," Mr. Holtzkemper added, "due to our brand-new exhaust system."

The heart of the '60 Buick's exhaust

Jim Whipple makes detailed inspection of new Wildcat engine

Transmission *Continued*

set-up is a single unique muffler located transversely between the frame rails and ahead of the gas tank. The one large muffler replaces two mufflers and two resonators found on the '59 Buicks.

The exhaust pipes enter each end of the muffler after a long, uniform run back from the exhaust manifolds. After passing through individual resonating chambers within the muffler, the gas impulses from right and left banks of cylinders are blended in a common chamber, then led through two more resonating chambers to a short tailpipe leading out under each fender.

This system has cut back pressure as much as twenty per cent, while at the same time lowering the noise level and eliminating much of the heat under the passenger compartment.

In the interest of further efficiency, more aluminum is used around the '60 Buick engine—in the generator mounting and end plates, on the front timing cover and water pump, and in the valve rocker arms. A worth-while weight saving of 57 pounds is the result of all the aluminum parts used in the engine.

But what impresses me most about the '60 Buick engines—even more than their terrific power—is their freedom from vibration throughout the entire speed range. From a soundless idle to full-throttle acceleration, these engines run with near electric motor smoothness.

The secret is very simple. Careful manufacture and inspection provides almost perfect engine balance. Pistons and connection rods are matched in weight to within a fraction of a gram. Finally, after complete assembly, each engine is balanced electronically while running under its own power.

Minute corrections are made by drilling to adjust the harmonic balancer on the front of the crankshaft.

Not only has this careful dynamic balancing knocked out fatigue-building vibration, but it permits the engine to rev up more freely and turn more easily, thus adding to acceleration potential and over-all output.

To sum it up, the '60 Buick's powerful and efficient V8 engine teamed with smooth-as-silk Turbine Drive makes one of the most effective power teams ever. installed in an American automobile.

Buick's extra-strong Box Girder K frame surrounds the car for unmatched security and protection. In the rear can be seen the revolutionary new Transverse Muffler

External styling changes for the 1961 Invicta were to be found in all areas. As seen from any angle, the new model was easily distinguishable. Some of the body types lost almost 200 lbs as a result of the changes. For instance, the four-door hardtop weighed 4,179 lbs, instead of 4,365 the year before.

Since the introduction of the Invicta, there had not been any change in its engine's output. The 401 cubic inch V-8 continued to develop 325 hp. That, in the somewhat lighter body was good for performance. This kind of Buick was gaining favor with Tom McCahill, Mechanix Illustrated's veteran car tester. He put a 1961 Invicta through its paces and got a 0 to 60 time of 8 seconds even. That was by starting in low and shifting to drive. By using drive without shifting, he got an 8.9 time, which was not bad, either. Top speed was 120 mph.

Invicta production was way down for 1961 to 28,733. That drop was because the Estate Wagons, both two- and three-seat models, were not available in the Invicta series. They were dropped down to the LeSabre line. Also, the Invicta four-door sedan was deleted. Only the convertible and the two hardtops could be ordered in the Invicta line.

There was a Custom option for the hardtops. It consisted of special leather upholstery in the four-door. For the two-door it included special vinyl upholstered bucket seats, a center storage console, and two-way power driver's seat.

Base prices were unchanged from the previous year. The range was from $3,447 for the two-door Sport Coupe to $3,620 for the convertible. There were 18,398 copies of the four-door hardtop built, or 64% of 1961 Invicta production. The 3,953 convertibles were the rarest Invicta body types of the model year.

No exclusive 1961 Invicta literature was issued. These models were included in the "full-size" Buick catalogue.

Detail styling changes were made to the Invicta for 1962. Evidently the public liked the result, because it was the best year for the super-powered, full-size Buicks since 1957. Invicta production practically doubled to 56,017.

That total included the Estate Wagons, which were returned to the Invicta level with resounding success. The two-seat model production totalled 9,131 and the three-seat model 4,617. Together, they amounted to 13,748—the most high-powered Buick station wagons to date. The most popular 1962 Invicta was the four-door hardtop, 16,443 built.

Surprisingly, the second-best selling body type was the convertible, of which an abundant 13,471 were produced.

Although the convertible's price was reduced $3 the hardtops were increased $152 for the four-door and $286 for the two-door. The Custom option was continued for the 1962 Invictas, and extended to the convertible. Estate Wagon prices were $3,827 and $3,917 for the six-passenger and eight-passenger models, respectively.

The engine was again unchanged with respect to its power. All Buick's engines were given the Wildcat name. For the Invicta (and Electras) it was called the Wildcat 445. The 445 referred the foot-pounds of torque it developed.

The Wildcat name was also used for a new model introduced during the model year. A second two-door hardtop was added. It was loaded with many items usually costing extra, like center console, vinyl covered roof, etc. The Wildcat had a tachometer as well, and used the same engine as the other Invicta models. Its weight was 4,150 lbs—about 75 more than the regular two-door Sport Coupe. At $3,927, it was the most costly Invicta model.

There were at least three brochures published to promote the new Wildcat and the compact Skylark together. The Invicta was included in the regular full-line catalogue, but the Wildcat model debuted too late to be included. After its introduction, the Wildcat was featured in several full-page magazine ads.

Literature excerpted for this chapter includes, for 1961, the main showroom catalogue (see pages 34-37). For 1962, two items are featured: the spring models catalogue entitled, "News about two hot new Buicks!" (see pages 38-41), and a Wilcat/Skylark folder entitled, "Buick makes the season's big news..." (see pages 42-47).

THE
CLEAN
LOOK
of action

THE BUICK INVICTA

". . . an automobile man's kind of automobile."

If an automotive engineer were asked to design a car for his own personal use, the chances are that the car would be a lot like the Buick Invicta. □ Engineers prize performance in a car, and Invicta offers performance aplenty. In fact, the Invicta with standard Wildcat 445 engine and Turbine Drive transmission is probably the best performing car built in America. □ Engineers like a smart-handling car, too, and the Invicta answers this requirement beautifully. It hugs the road, stays tight on the curves and corners, and stops practically on a dime with its big, fin-cooled brakes. □ And an engineer—like everyone else—appreciates a smartly-styled and smartly-appointed car. Invicta, beautiful inside and out, bears Buick's own unmistakable brand of elegance. □ While Invicta is truly an automobile man's kind of automobile, it's a car for anyone who enjoys high-spirited motoring.

Invicta Standard Equipment: Turbine Drive transmission • Electric clock • Automatic trunk light • Deluxe steering wheel • Custom Padded Cushions • License plate frame • Mirromagic instrument panel • Direction signals • Fin-cooled brakes with aluminum front drums • Full-flow oil filter • Electric windshield wipers • Automatic glove compartment light • Trip mileage indicator • Electric cigarette lighter • Dual sunshades • StepOn parking brake • Magic Mirror finish • Deluxe wheel covers • Two-way power driver's seat on **custom** two-door hardtop • Storage console on **custom** two-door hardtop • Front and rear fold-down armrests on the **Invicta custom** four-door hardtop.

The Buick Invicta Convertible

There's a youthful zest about this custom Invicta interior*, with the luxury overtones of genuine leather. This is the **Invicta Custom** 4-door hardtop with seat cushions and backs in supple, top-grain leathers and extra convenient pull-down center armrests in front and rear seats.

INVICTA

The Buick Invicta 4-Door Hardtop

Invicta's standard interior bears all the signs of
Buick elegance. This Invicta 2-door hardtop
features Braeburn cloth in a smart striped
pattern, luxuriously matched with "Jewel-Tone"
vinyl. Convertible interior trims are available
in six beautiful all-vinyl combinations.

INVICTA CUSTOM

Sports car flair is the hallmark of
this **Invicta Custom** 2-door
hardtop interior*. Front seats are the
"bucket" type in harmonizing
shades of "Jewel-Tone" vinyl.
Between front seats is a
handy storage console upholstered
in matching vinyl . . . perfect
for storing so many small
travel needs. Two-way
power driver's seat standard.

*Custom interiors op-
tional at extra cost.

BUICK'S UNLEASHED A *w...*

...THE NEW FULL-SIZ...

CUSTOM EQUIPMENT at no extra cost! All of these comfort and convenience features are included as standard equipment on Wildcat: Turbine Drive Transmission • 325-Horsepower Wildcat 445 Engine • Heater and Defroster • Rear Seat Speaker • Foam-padded Bucket Front Seats • Electric Clock • Deluxe Steer-

ing Wheel •
Frame • Al...
Windshield ...
strument Pan...
All-Vinyl Fro...
lining and S...

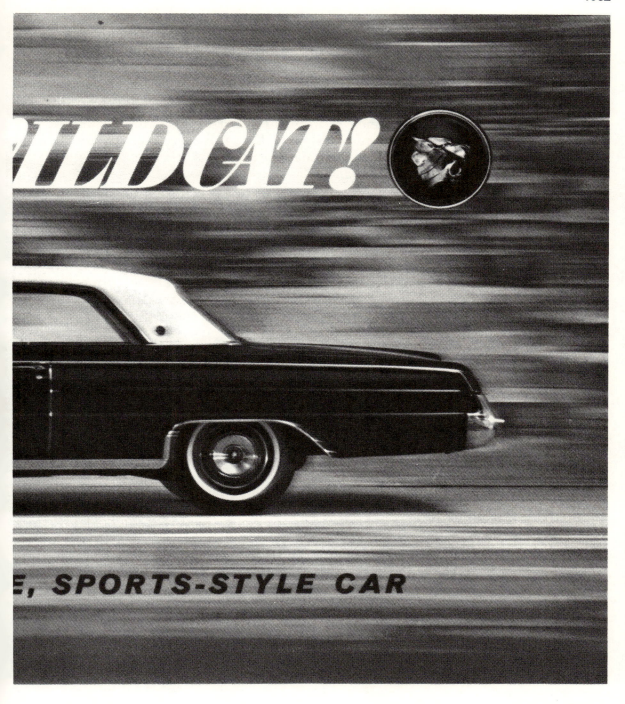

WILDCAT!

E, SPORTS-STYLE CAR

Automatic Trunk Light • License Plate minum Front Brake Drums • Electric pers • Step-On Parking Brake • In- Safety Pad • Directional Signals • Bucket Seats • Foam Rubber Head- Shades • Chrome-plated Roof Bows • Center Console • Tachometer • Console-mounted Transmission Selector Lever • Carpeting • Custom Top Covering • Wildcat Wheel Covers • Rear Floor Area Courtesy Light (mounted at rear of console) • Dual Exhaust • Full 15-inch Wheels • Custom Bright Exterior Mouldings.

The Buick Wildcat is an entirely new idea in driving pleasure. It combines the verve of sports-car styling, handling characteristics and power with the comfortable roominess of a full-size family car. Make no mistake, the Wildcat is designed strictly for American driving. It has the same built-in quality and reliability of other full-size 1962 Buicks . . . yet Buick Wildcat offers you thrilling sports-car styling and driving not to be found in other full-size cars.

SPORTS-CAR WALLOP—A standard-equipment, four-barrel Wildcat V-8 engine puts 325 horsepower at your command for booming get-up-and-go lightning-like passing acceleration.

SPORTS-CAR HANDLING—You get arrow-straight tracking, even in cross-winds, and precision cornering, because the front wheels carry more of the car weight. Advanced Thrust design has accomplished this by moving the engine forward and positioning it over the front wheels.

SAFE, SURE STOPS EVERY TIME—Buick's superior brakes have been described as "the best in the industry." Here's why: stop-and-go driving builds up heat in brake drums—Buick's fin-cooled *aluminum* drums "soak up"—and get rid of—heat faster. The going's safer—brake linings last longer, and maintenance costs less.

SPORTS-CAR STYLING—On the inside, contoured bucket seats in rugged Seville-grain vinyl and a center console with tachometer are standard equipment on the new Wildcat. Turbine Drive shift lever is mounted in the console. Chrome roof bows accent the headlining. Headlining is foam rubber, making Buick's famous quiet ride even quieter. On the outside, a white or black vinyl sheath for the crisp Landau top is standard equipment. You can select *your* exterior finish from among 15 exciting colors.

FULL-SIZE BUICK ROOMINESS AND COMFORT—Just like other full-size Buicks, the new Wildcat has man-size headroom, front and back. There's "stretch-out" legroom for the front seat passenger and, with contoured bucket seats, all the comfort of your favorite easy chair. And in the back seat, there's ample knee room for six-footers.

See us—Try the exciting New Wildcat

Bucket seats available in Fawn, Red, Blue, and White vinyl.

Illuminated tachometer shows
engine operating rpm's.

Center console provides storage space
between driver and front seat passenger.

for yourself! / HERE'S MORE EXCITING NEWS FROM BUICK!

THINGS YOU SHOULD KNOW ABOUT
THE BUICK *WILDCAT!*

STANDARD EQUIPMENT

Turbine Drive Transmission • 325 Horsepower Wildcat 445 Engine • Heater and Defroster • Rear Seat Speaker • Foam-Padded Seats—Front and Rear • Electric Clock • Deluxe Steering Wheel • Automatic Trunk Light • License Plate Frame • Aluminum Front Brake Drums • Full-flow Oil Filter • Re-usable Air cleaner Element • Electric Windshield Wipers • Step-On Parking Brake • Instrument Panel Safety Pad • Directional Signals • Glove Compartment Light • Smoking Set • Rear Seat Ash Trays • Dual Sun Shades • Dual Arm Rests—Front and Rear • Five 7.60 x 15 Tubeless Tires • All Vinyl Front Bucket Seats • Foam Rubber Headlining • Center Console • Tachometer • Console-mounted Transmission Selector Lever • Carpeting • Wildcat Wheel Covers • Custom Top Covering • Rear Floor Area Courtesy Light (mounted at rear of console) • Dual Exhaust • Dual Horns • Full 15-in. Wheels • Single Key Locking System • Key Starting • Crank-operated Front Window Vents • Distinctive Wildcat Exterior Trim

OPTIONS AND ACCESSORIES

Power Steering • Sonomatic Radio and Manual Antenna • Sonomatic Radio with Electric Antenna • Wonderbar Radio with Manual Antenna • Wonderbar Radio with Electric Antenna • Safety Group (Back up Lights, Glare Proof Mirror, Parking Brake Signal Light, Safety Buzzer, Trip Odometer and Courtesy Lights) • Windshield Washer—Dual Speed Wiper • Soft Ray Tinted Glass (Windshield Only) • Power Brakes • Soft Ray Tinted Glass (all windows) • Deluxe Handy Mats • Deluxe Carpet Saver • Carpet Covers • Trunk Mat • Air Conditioner • Air Conditioner Modification • Chrome Door Guards • Twilight Sentinel • Remote Control Side View Mirror • Whitewall Tires • Oversize Whitewall Tires • Oversize Blackwall Tires • Power Windows • Positive Crankcase Ventilation • Guide Matic • Positive Traction Differential • Automatic Trunk Release • Gas Tank Door Guard • Compass • Tissue Dispenser • Spotlamp • Rear Window Defroster • Outside Rearview Mirror • Vision Vanity Mirror • Map Case Package • Seat Belts

SPECIFICATIONS

Engine: Wildcat 445; Type: 90°V8; Displacement, cu. in.: 401; Horsepower @ 4400 R.P.M.: 325; Max. Torque: 445 @ 2800 R.P.M.; Compression Ratio: 10.25 to 1; Carburetor: 4-Barrel; Transmission: Turbine Drive. Engine lubricating System: Main bearings, connecting rods and camshaft bearings pressure lubricated. Piston pins splash lubricated. Cylinder walls splash and nozzle lubricated. Normal oil pressure 40 @ 1600 r.p.m. Full-flow oil filter standard on all models. Crankcase capacity (refill less filter): 4 quarts. Fuel System: Four-barrel carburetor. Standard automatic choke. Mechanical fuel pump. Two stage gasoline filter with fine filter in fuel tank and extra-fine filter at the carburetor. Oil-impregnated polyurethane air cleaner. Exhaust-type intake manifold heat control. Twenty-gallon fuel capacity. Engine Cooling: Pressure system. Choke-type circulation thermostat. Centrifugal water pump. Capacity: 18.5 quarts with heater. Exhaust System: Single muffler for both banks of cylinders is mounted crosswise to the frame. Heavy zinc and aluminum coatings of muffler parts promote long life. Dual exhaust standard. Electrical: Twelve-volt electrical system. Five-position starter-ignition switch. Transmission: Turbine Drive standard. Turbine Drive is a torque converter type of transmission, fully automatic with two turbines, a variable-pitch stator and a fixed-vane stator. Maximum torque ratio in DRIVE range at stall, 3.4 to 1. Total oil capacity (refill): 12 quarts. Propeller Shaft: Hide-Away Drive Shaft is slightly angled to reduce tunnel height in rear seat. Angled sections are connected by a special constant-velocity universal joint that insures vibrationless transfer of power to rear axle. Shaft is connected to transmission and rear axle by needle bearing universal joints. Rear Axle: Hypoid gears, semi-floating. Gear ratios with Wildcat 445, 3.23 to 1. Rear wheel bearings permanently lubricated. Transfer of driving forces through rubber-mounted arms connected to frame. Positive traction differential optional. Frame: Safety-X-Frame with box section cross-members and tubular center section through which propeller shaft passes. Extra-heavy body side rails add extra strength. Suspension: Independent ball-joint front suspension with link-type stabilizer bar. Three-link-type rear suspension with track bar. Coil springs front and rear. Rear springs loaded through lower control arms. Direct acting hydraulic shock absorbers front and rear. New suspension geometry means there's no "squat" when you start, no "dive" when you stop. Brakes: Hydraulic, self energizing. Air-cooled finned, aluminum brake drums front; finned cast iron drums rear. Total lining area: 197.32 sq. in. Step-On parking brake operating through rear service brake shoes. Power brakes optional. Wheels and Tires: Disc-type wheels. Size 6.00″ x 15″, "L"-type flange. Tires: 7.60″ x 15″; Oversize tires optional, Whitewall tires optional. Steering: Easy Power Steering optional. Overall ratio: 20.7 to 1. Flexible coupling in power gear screens out vibration. Exterior Dimensions: Overall Length: 214.1″; Overall Width: 77.9″; Overall Height: 56.4″; Wheelbase: 123.0″; Tread—Front: 62.0″; Tread—Rear: 61.0″. Interior Dimensions: Leg Room, Front: 44.5″; Leg Room, Rear: 38.8″; Head Room, Front: 37.8″*; Head Room, Rear: 38.3″*; Shoulder Room, Front: 58.9″; Shoulder Room, Rear: 56.9″.

*Depressed

THE LUXURY OF A BUICK with the zest and flair of a sports car. That's the interior of the brilliant new Buick Wildcat.

SPORTS CAR TOUCHES IN A SETTING OF LUXURY...BUICK WILDCAT

RICHLY-STYLED BUCKET SEATS in a smart selection of leather-grained vinyls set a sporty tone for the Buick Wildcat interior.

FOAM RUBBER HEAD LINING is a pleasure to look at, a pleasure to touch. Makes a big contribution, too, to Wildcat quietness.

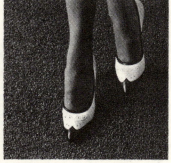

DEEP CARPETING, color-keyed to Wildcat interior decor, puts extra luxury underfoot. Thick, durable weave means long life and good looks.

RALLYIST'S TACHOMETER set in a handsome console between the seats is a never-ending delight for performance lovers. Standard equipment.

BRIGHT METAL CONSOLE between front seats contains Turbine Drive control and indicator as well as tachometer. Standard equipment.

REAR SEAT COURTESY LIGHT is mounted on the back of the console for extra safety and convenience. Lights when door is opened.

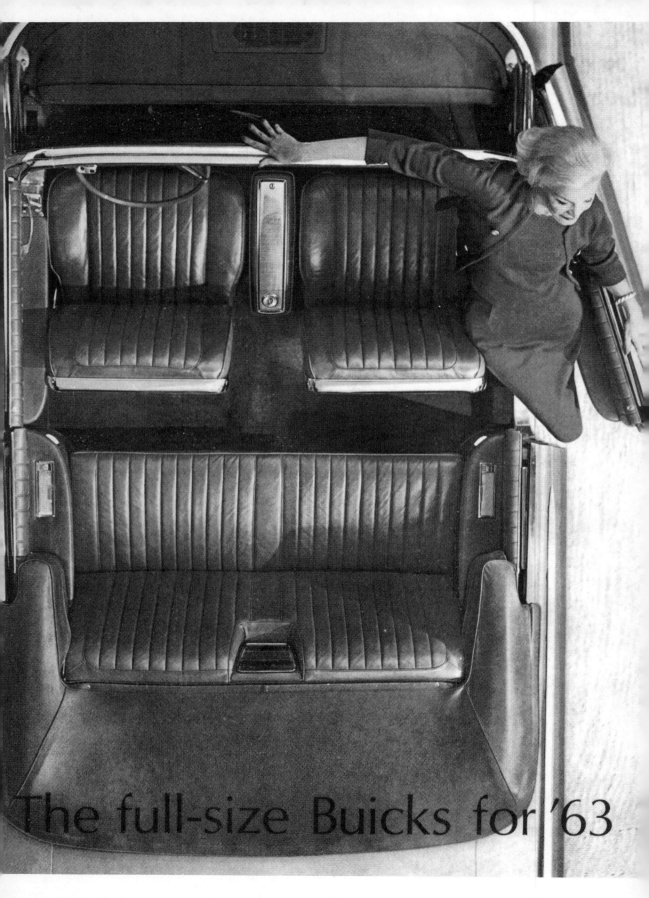

The full-size Buicks for '63

The Wildcat name was much more exciting than Invicta, so the 1963 models were called Wildcat, except the Estate Wagon. It retained the Invicta title, but 1963 was the last year it was used.

Wildcat came in three body types—two hardtops and a convertible. The price of the two-door Sport Coupe was down $78 to $3,849. The four-door hardtop sold for $3,871 and the convertible was $3,961. The Invicta Estate Wagon was priced at $3,969 for the two-seat model.

There was no three-seat Estate Wagon after 1962, and only 3,495 Invicta two-seat wagons were built for 1963. The rarest Wildcat of the year was the convertible. The 6,021 total was down disastrously the previous year's Invicta convertible production. The best selling Wildcat was the two-door Sport Coupe. The 17,519 built account for practically half the model year's Wildcat production. Wildcat popularity was not overwhelming during its first full model year, but neither was it a great disappointment.

Top speed was reported by the "World Car Catalog" to be 120 mph. Wildcat power came from the Wildcat engine. It was virtually the same 401 cubic inch displacement 325 hp V-8 that was found under the hood of every Invicta. Incidentally, total Invicta production (including the 1962 Wildcats) amounted to 186,507 high-performance cars.

The big 1963 Buick catalogue, and the slightly smaller "full-size" catalogue, included the Wildcat and Invicta. There was no literature issued just on the Wildcat. It was featured in magazine ads, however.

Although the redesigned bodies were about 3 inches longer for 1964, they were somewhat lighter. The Wildcat 2-door Sport Coupe tipped the scales at just 3 lbs over the two ton mark. As had been the tradition with the Century and Invicta, the Wildcat used the same body as the smallest full-size Buick. However, this year the Wildcat initiated detail distinctions. It had its own grille, extra chrome just above the sill and three chrome darts on the front fenders.

The Estate Wagon was deleted from the Wildcat line-up, like it had been removed from the Invicta series two years earlier. The Wildcat models and their prices for 1964 were: four-door sedan, $3,164; two-door Sport Coupe, $3,267; four-door hardtop, $3,327; and convertible, $3,455.

Convertible production of 7,850 was substantial for the line's rarest model. Wildcat's most popular model was the four-door hardtop. With 33,358 units built, it almost equalled total Wildcat production in the 1963 model year. Overall Wildcat production for 1964 shot up 136% to 84,245 cars.

The main reason that made the Wildcat such a hot selling car was its hot performance. Although the familiar 325 hp engine was standard, another break from tradition was the availability of optional power. Not just one, but two, optional V-8s could be ordered in the 1964 Wildcat. The Wildcat 465 engine was a 425 cubic inch displacement V-8 that developed 340 hp. It was the Riviera's standard engine. The Super Wildcat engine was similar, but with two 4-barrel carburetors that produced 360 advertised hp. The extra cost for these engines was a modest $48 and $188, respectively. The Wildcat sedan with the Super Wildcat V-8 weighed just over 11 lbs per hp, compared to over 17½ for the standard 1964 LeSabre sedan.

There was also a transmission choice in the 1964 Wildcat. A 3-speed manual was standard, but a 4-speed manual or Super Turbine 400 automatic could be ordered instead.

Wildcat was included in the all-series Buick catalogues for the year. No exclusive Wildcat literature is known to have been published. With a top speed of 120 mph, Wildcat's magazine advertising was understandably aimed at the performance minded buyers.

Literature excerpted for this chapter includes the 1963 large showroom catalogue (see pages 48 and 50-59) and the similar 1964 item (see pages 60-68).

Buick's liveliest

As its name suggests, the Wildcat is the star among Buick performers. In fact, we think you'll find the Wildcat one of the liveliest cars you've ever driven. Along with its sports car performance, there's a beguiling sports car look and feel, unusual in a full-size car. For instance, in bucket-seat models the automatic Turbine Drive selector and engine tachometer are mounted on a smart storage console between the front seats. High-performance 4-speed synchromesh transmission is optional on all three models of the lively '63 Buick Wildcat Series.

The Wildcat

THE BUICK WILDCAT CONVERTIBLE

Buick Wildcat Standard Equipment

Wildcat V8 engine (325 hp.) • Automatic Turbine Drive transmission • Foam-padded bucket seats (except four-door hardtop) • Electric clock • Deluxe steering wheel • Automatic trunk light • License plate frame • Air-cooled brakes with aluminum front drums • Full-flow oil filter • Electric windshield wipers • Instrument panel padding • Direction signals • Glove compartment light • Foam-rubber headlining (except convertible) • Center console (except 4-door hardtop with bench-type seats) • Illuminated tachometer (except 4-door hardtop with bench-type seats) • Console-mounted transmission selector lever (except 4-door hardtop with bench-type seats) • Rear floor area courtesy light (except 4-door hardtop with bench-type seats) • Carpeting front and rear • Wildcat wheel covers • Dual exhausts.

The look of luxury is what catches your eye in this Wildcat 4-door hardtop with conventional front seats. Pull-down arm rest is standard equipment. Bucket seats are optional at extra cost in this model.

Buick's liveliest . . . the Wildcat

THE BUICK WILDCAT 4-DOOR HARDTOP

THE BUICK WILDCAT 2-DOOR SPORT COUPE

Focal point of this sporty Wildcat Custom 4-door hardtop interior is the smart console between the front seats. It contains an illuminated tachometer, automatic Turbine Drive selector lever and storage compartment. The bucket seats are upholstered in soft vinyl that's wonderfully easy to clean and keep clean. (Bucket seats are standard on the Wildcat convertible and sport coupe.)

The Buick Wildcat Engines *(and what makes them purr)*

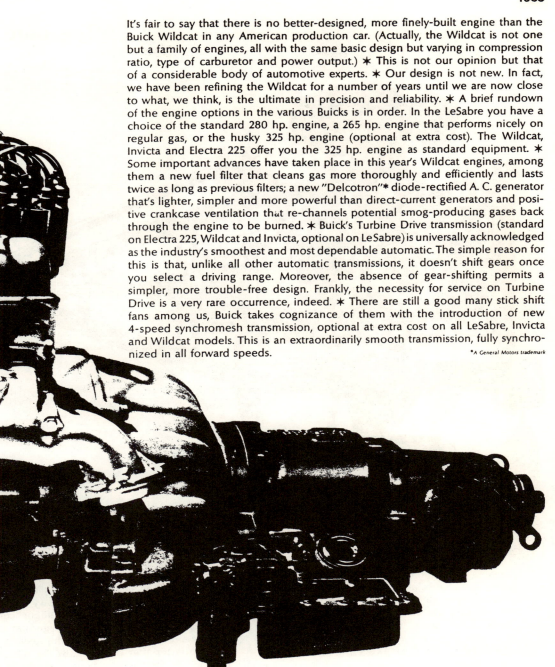

It's fair to say that there is no better-designed, more finely-built engine than the Buick Wildcat in any American production car. (Actually, the Wildcat is not one but a family of engines, all with the same basic design but varying in compression ratio, type of carburetor and power output.) ✻ This is not our opinion but that of a considerable body of automotive experts. ✻ Our design is not new. In fact, we have been refining the Wildcat for a number of years until we are now close to what, we think, is the ultimate in precision and reliability. ✻ A brief rundown of the engine options in the various Buicks is in order. In the LeSabre you have a choice of the standard 280 hp. engine, a 265 hp. engine that performs nicely on regular gas, or the husky 325 hp. engine (optional at extra cost). The Wildcat, Invicta and Electra 225 offer you the 325 hp. engine as standard equipment. ✻ Some important advances have taken place in this year's Wildcat engines, among them a new fuel filter that cleans gas more thoroughly and efficiently and lasts twice as long as previous filters; a new "Delcotron"✻ diode-rectified A. C. generator that's lighter, simpler and more powerful than direct-current generators and positive crankcase ventilation that re-channels potential smog-producing gases back through the engine to be burned. ✻ Buick's Turbine Drive transmission (standard on Electra 225, Wildcat and Invicta, optional on LeSabre) is universally acknowledged as the industry's smoothest and most dependable automatic. The simple reason for this is that, unlike all other automatic transmissions, it doesn't shift gears once you select a driving range. Moreover, the absence of gear-shifting permits a simpler, more trouble-free design. Frankly, the necessity for service on Turbine Drive is a very rare occurrence, indeed. ✻ There are still a good many stick shift fans among us, Buick takes cognizance of them with the introduction of new 4-speed synchromesh transmission, optional at extra cost on all LeSabre, Invicta and Wildcat models. This is an extraordinarily smooth transmission, fully synchronized in all forward speeds.

*A General Motors trademark

The bare facts

1. **6,000-mile lubrication** It takes six months of average driving before a 1963 Buick needs a chassis lubrication job. We're using a special premium chassis lubricant that protects the Buick suspension system better and longer—gives you a cushiony ride up to six times as long as ordinary chassis grease, and saves you money, too.

2. **Self-adjusting brakes** The brake pedal is always safely right up to the top with Buick's new self-adjusting brakes. Each time you apply the brakes while traveling in reverse, adjustments are automatically made. It's another improvement in Buick's bigger, better brakes which include front drums of fast-cooling aluminum at no extra cost.

3. **Advanced Thrust design** Buick moved both engine and transmission farther forward to accomplish a two-fold purpose: (1) flatten the front-seat floor, and (2) make handling surer and more positive, particularly in heavy crosswinds. Along with this forward movement comes a brand-new front suspension design that adds to this steadiness . . . even makes the steering wheel return faster after cornering. By the way, Buick's floors are the flattest among all full-size American cars. Any seat in a 1963 Buick is a good seat.

4. **Full-coil suspension** Buick puts a husky coil spring at each wheel to soak up bumps and road shock. Unlike leaf springs, coil springs are

# of Buick quality

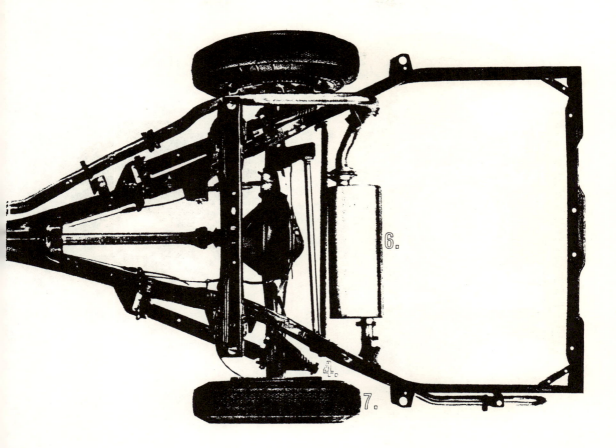

unaffected by the action of dirt, water, salt and slush. They stay permanently resilient. Shock absorber adjustments need not be changed periodically to compensate for decreases in spring effectiveness. It's always smooth sailing in a Buick.

5. Safety-X-Frame Here's the foundation of Buick's solid, stable ride. Massive tubular sections of steel are welded in an "X" shape for maximum strength and rigidity. Joined to the extra-heavy siderails in the Buick body, this X-frame forms triangular sections that offer tremendous impact resistance for the ultimate in family safety.

6. Aluminized muffler Buick's famous single transverse muffler is now made of aluminized steel for premium corrosion resistance and long, long life. Another important muffler life-extender is the new simplified design that greatly reduces the number of parts.

Dual exhaust system is standard on Wildcat models, optional at extra cost on all other full-size Buicks except Le Sabre and Invicta Estate Wagons.

7. 15-inch wheels Buick is one of the few American cars to give you full 15-inch wheels as standard equipment. These bigger wheels carry bigger tires that make fewer revolutions for every mile of travel . . . run cooler and last longer. Brakes are bigger, too, for greater stopping power.

ENGINES

Available On	LeSabre** (regular gas)	LeSabre (standard)	LeSabre* Wildcat Invicta Electra 225
Type	90° V8	90° V8	90° V8
Displacement Cu. in.	401	401	401
Horsepower @ 4400 R. P. M.	265	280	325
Max. Torque	412	424	445
Compression Ratio	9.0 to 1	10.25 to 1	10.25 to 1
Carburetor	2-Barrel	2-Barrel	4-Barrel
Transmission	3-Speed Synch.	3-Speed Synch.	Turbine Drive

*Optional at extra cost **Optional at no extra cost

Engine Lubricating System: Main bearings, connecting rods and camshaft bearings pressure lubricated. Piston pins splash lubricated. Cylinder walls splash and nozzle lubricated. Normal oil pressure 40 at 2400 rpm. Full-flow oil filter standard on all models. Crankcase capacity (refill less filter): 4 quarts. **Fuel System:** Two- or four-barrel carburetor according to engine chart above. Standard automatic choke. Mechanical fuel pump. Two-stage gasoline filter with fine filter in fuel tank. Oil-impregnated polyurethane air cleaner. Exhaust-type intake manifold heat control. Twenty-gallon fuel capacity. **Engine Cooling:** Pressure system. Choke-type circulation thermostat. Centrifugal water pump. Capacity: 18.5 quarts with heater. **Exhaust System:** Single muffler for both banks of cylinders is mounted crosswise to the frame. Constructed of corrosion resistant aluminized steel to promote longer life. Dual exhaust standard on Wildcat models, optional on all others. (Not available on Estate Wagons.) **Electrical:** Twelve-volt electrical system. Five-position starter-ignition switch. **Transmission:** Turbine Drive standard on Invicta Estate Wagon, Wildcat and Electra 225. Turbine Drive is a torque converter type of transmission, fully automatic with two turbines, a variable-pitch stator and a fixed-vane stator. Maximum torque ratio in DRIVE range at stall 3.4 to 1. Total oil capacity (refill): 12 quarts. **Propeller Shaft:** Drive Shaft is slightly angled to reduce tunnel height in rear seat. Angled sections are connected by a special constant-velocity universal joint that insures vibrationless transfer of power to rear axle. Shaft is connected to transmission and rear axle by needle bearing universal joints. **Rear Axle:** Hypoid gears, semi-floating. Gear ratios for 265 and 280 horsepower engine. 3.36 to 1 with synchromesh transmission, 2.78 to 1 with Turbine Drive; with 325 horsepower engine, 3.23 to 1. Rear wheel bearings permanently lubricated. Transfer of driving forces through rubber-mounted arms connected to frame. Positive traction differential optional on all models. **Frame:** Safety-X-Frame with box-section crossmembers and tubular center section through which propeller shaft passes. Extra-heavy body side rails add extra strength. **Suspension:** Independent ball-joint front suspension with link-type stabilizer bar. Three-link-type rear suspension with track bar. Coil springs front and rear. Rear springs loaded through lower control arms. Direct acting hydraulic shock absorbers front and rear. New suspension geometry means there's no "squat" when

you start, no "dive" when you stop. **Brakes:** Hydraulic, self-energizing. Air-cooled finned, aluminum brake drums front; finned cast iron drums rear. Total lining area: 197.32 sq. in. Step-on parking brake operating through rear service brake shoes. Power brakes standard on Electra 225, optional on Invicta, Wildcat and LeSabre. **Wheels and Tires:** Disc-type wheels. Size: 15" x 6.00", "L"-type flange. Tires: LeSabre, Wildcat and Invicta, 7.60" x 15"; Electra 225, 8.00" x 15". Oversize tires optional on Wildcat. Whitewall tires optional on all models. **Steering:** Manual recirculating ball steering standard on LeSabre, Invicta and Wildcat. Overall ratio: 33.0 to 1. Easy Power Steering standard on Electra 225; optional on Invicta, Wildcat and LeSabre. Overall ratio: 20.5 to 1. Flexible coupling in power gear screens out vibration.

†Note: Models 4639, 4647, and 4667 have a 3.42 to 1 rear axle ratio. When a 4400 series, 4635 or 4800 series car is equipped with a 4-speed synchromesh transmission it will also have a 3.42 to 1 rear axle ratio.

EXTERIOR DIMENSIONS	LeSabre	Wildcat	Electra 225	LeSabre Invicta Estate Wagons
Overall Length	215.7	215.7	221.7	215.7
Overall Width	78.0	78.0	78.0	78.0
Overall Height	56.7	55.6	57.5	*
Wheelbase	123	123	126	123
Tread—Front	62	62	62	62
Tread—Rear	61	61	61	61

INTERIOR DIMENSIONS	Leg Room Front	Leg Room Rear	Head Room Front	Head Room Rear	Shoulder Room Front	Shoulder Room Rear
LeSABRE						
2-dr. Sedan	*	*	*	*	*	*
2-dr. Sport Cpe.	40.2	35.8	*	*	58.7	57.8
4-dr. H-top	40.5	38.2	38.0	37.6	58.8	58.0
4-dr. Sedan	40.5	38.2	38.8	37.6	58.8	58.0
Estate Wagons	*	*	*	*	*	*
Convertible	*	*	*	*	*	*
INVICTA						
Estate Wagon	*	*	*	*	*	*
WILDCAT						
4-dr. H-top	40.5	37.5	38.0	37.6	58.8	58.0
2-dr. Sport Cpe.	40.0	37.5	37.8	37.6	58.9	58.0
Convertible	41.1	35.7	39.1	38.0	58.9	51.5
ELECTRA 225						
4-dr. Sedan 4819	40.7	41.2	39.5	38.6	58.7	57.3
2-dr. Sport Cpe. 4847	40.4	38.6	38.0	38.1	58.6	57.4
4-dr. H-top 4839	40.6	39.0	38.1	38.0	58.7	58.1
4-dr., 6-window 4829 H-top, Sedan	40.6	41.2	39.5	38.6	58.7	58.0
Convertible 4867	40.4	38.7	39.0	37.9	58.6	51.4

*Not available at time of printing.

Buick Motor Division, General Motors Corporation, reserves the right to make changes at any time, without notice, in prices, colors, materials, equipment, specifications and models, and also to discontinue models.

BUICK MOTOR DIVISION, GENERAL MOTORS CORPORATION, FLINT 2, MICHIGAN

Illustrated: The **Buick Wildcat Sport Coupe** with optional custom fabric roof cover and optional "Formula Five" chrome-plated steel wheels.

This is the Buick **WILDCAT!** The regular engine
is 325 horsepower with options up to
360. This should suggest something
to you about Wildcat performance. Fifteen minutes at the wheel
will suggest a lot more. Fun lovers of the world may now rally 'round.

WILDCAT!

Wildcat comes equipped with the following at no extra charge: 3-Speed Synchromesh Transmission □ 325 Horsepower Wildcat 445 Engine □ Aluminum Front Brake Drums □ Full-flow Oil Filter □ Re-usable Air Cleaner Element □ Electric Windshield Wipers □ StepOn Parking Brake □ Upper Instrument Panel Safety Pad □ Directional Signals □ Glove Compartment Light □ Smoking Set □ Rear Seat Ash Trays □ Magic Mirror Finish □ Dual Arm Rests—Front and Rear □ Five 7.60 x 15 Tubeless Tires □ Carpeting □ Wildcat Wheel Covers □ Single, Transverse Muffler □ Dual Horns □ Full 15-inch Wheels □ Single-Key Locking System □ Crank-Operated Front Window Vents □ 6,000 Mile Lubed Front Suspension □ Delcotron Generator □ Self-adjusting Brakes □ Positive Crankcase Ventilation □ Front-door-operated dome light. □ □ □ □ □

WILDCAT!

Next best thing to owning a Riviera! This is the bucket-seat luxury available in the Wild-cat Sport Coupe, 4-door hardtop and convertible. The upholstery is in vinyl so soft and supple you'd swear it was real leather. Between the front seats is a smart console with storage space, ash tray and Super Turbine "400" selector. An illuminated tachometer that allows you to track the performance of the great Wildcat engine is available at extra cost.

THE WILDCAT 4-DOOR HARDTOP. Note the distinctive treatment of the traditional Buick venti-ports. Like all Wildcats this year, this one is available with "Formula Five" chrome-plated steel wheels.

THE WILDCAT CONVERTIBLE. The Wildcat is as dazzling going away as it is coming. Take a good look at the beautifully integrated rear-end treatment with smart chrome bars between the taillights. By the way, there's a mighty big trunk beneath that gleaming deck lid. Optional "Formula Five" wheel shown.

THE WILDCAT 4-DOOR SEDAN. Here's a look at the Wildcat's distinctively sporty grille. Its heavy die-cast chrome wings with a tri-shield in the center seem to float against a background of smaller chrome bars. For maximum smoothness, you'll probably want Super Turbine 400 automatic transmission on your Wildcat.

(Left) If you prefer the bench-type seat with the custom look, it's yours in luxurious expanded vinyl, so soft and supple it looks and feels like real leather. This is the interior of a Wildcat 4-door hardtop, a wonderfully luxurious and spirited car with such refinements as a fold down center, armrests—front and rear—for long-distance driver and passenger comfort. Wildcat for '64 offers a wide variety of custom and regular interior trims.

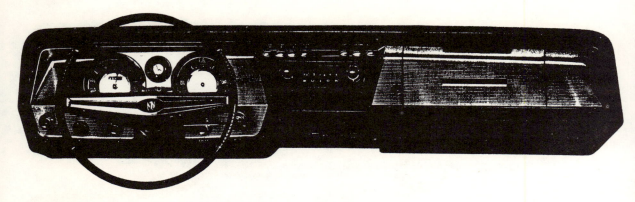

SPECIFICATIONS: LeSabre □ Wildcat □ Electra 225 □ Riviera

ENGINE

		Horse-power	Torque	Com-pression Ratio	Displace-ment (cu. ins.)	Car-buretion	Fuel
LeSabre	Wildcat 310*	210 @ 4600	310 @ 2400	9.0 to 1	300	2-barrel	Regular
Wildcat	Wildcat 445	325 @ 4400	445 @ 2800	10.25 to 1	401	4-barrel	Premium
Electra 225	Wildcat 445	325 @ 4400	445 @ 2800	10.25 to 1	401	4-barrel	Premium
Riviera	Wildcat 465	340 @ 4400	465 @ 2800	10.25 to 1	425	4-barrel	Premium

*Except LeSabre Estate Wagons which have the Wildcat 445.

ENGINE OPTIONS

	Horse-power	Torque	Com-pression Ratio	Displace-ment	Car-buretion	Fuel	Availability
Wildcat 355	250	335 @ 3000	11.0 to 1	300	4-barrel	Prem.	All LeSabres except Estate Wagons
Wildcat 465	340	465 @ 2800	10.25 to 1	425	4-barrel	Prem.	Wildcat, Electra 225 and LeSabre Estate Wagons
Super Wildcat	360	465 @ 2800	10.25 to 1	425	2, 4-bbl.	Prem.	Wildcat, Electra 225, Riviera and LeSabre Estate Wagons

TRANSMISSIONS

	Regular Equipment	Option (Manual)	Option (Automatic)
LeSabre	3-Speed Synchro.	4-Speed Synchro.	Super Turbine 300* & 400
Wildcat	3-Speed Synchro.	4-Speed Synchro.	Super Turbine 400
Electra 225	Super Turbine 400	None	None
Riviera	Super Turbine 400	None	None

*LeSabre Estate Wagons will use Super Turbine 400.

REAR AXLE RATIOS

	3-Speed Manual Trans.	4-Speed Manual Trans.	Super Turbine 300	Super Turbine 400
LeSabre	3.42	3.42	3.07	3.07
Wildcat	3.23	3.42	—	3.07
Electra 225	—	—	—	3.07
Riviera	—	—	—	3.07

Engine Lubricating System: Main bearings, connecting rods and camshaft bearings pressure lubricated. Cylinder walls splash and nozzle lubricated. Normal oil pressure 33 @ 2400 (LeSabre except Estate Wagons); 40 @ 2400 (Wildcat, Electra 225, Riviera and LeSabre Estate Wagons). Full-flow oil filter. Crankcase capacity (refill less filter) 4 quarts. **Fuel System:** Automatic choke. Mechanical fuel pump. Two-stage gasoline filter with fine filter in fuel tank. Oil-impregnated polyurethane air cleaner. Exhaust type intake manifold heat control (Wildcat, Electra 225, Riviera and LeSabre Estate Wagons). Water-type intake manifold heat control on all LeSabres except Estate Wagons. Twenty gallon fuel capacity. **Engine Cooling:** Pressure system. Choke-type circulation thermostat. Centrifugal water pump. Capacity: 401 cubic inches is 18.5 quarts, 300 cubic inches is 13.7 quarts, with heater. **Exhaust System:** Single muffler for both banks of cylinders is mounted crosswise to the frame. Constructed of corrosion resistant aluminized steel to promote longer life. Dual exhausts available as optional equipment on all models except Estate Wagons. **Electrical:** Twelve volt electrical system. Five-position starter-ignition switch. **Automatic Transmissions:** Super Turbine 300 is a torque converter type featuring a variable pitch stator within the converter; and single planetary gear set. Maximum torque ratio in DRIVE range at

stall 2.45. Total oil capacity (refill) 18.5 pints. Super Turbine 400 is a torque converter type with a double planetary gear arrangement. Maximum torque ratio in DRIVE range at stall 2.10. Total oil capacity (refill) 22 pints. **Propeller Shaft:** Drive shaft is slightly angled to reduce tunnel height in rear seat. Angled sections are connected by a special constant-velocity universal joint that insures vibrationless transfer of power to rear axle. Shaft is connected to transmission and rear axle by needle bearing universal joints. **Rear Axle:** Hypoid gears, semi-floating. Transfer of driving forces through rubber-mounted arms connected to frame. Positive traction differential optional on all models. **Frame:** Safety-X-Frame with box section cross-members and tubular center section through which propeller shaft passes. **Suspension:** Independent ball-joint front suspension with link-type stabilizer bar. Three-link-type rear suspension with track bar. Coil springs front and rear. Rear springs loaded through lower control arms. Direct acting hydraulic shock absorbers front and rear. **Brakes:** Hydraulic, self-energizing. Air-cooled finned, aluminum brake drums front; finned cast iron drums rear. Total lining area: 197.32 sq. in. Step-on parking brake operating through rear service brake shoes. Power brakes standard on Electra 225 and Riviera, optional on Wildcat and LeSabre. **Wheels and Tires:** Disc-type wheels. 15 x 5:50 "K" on LeSabre. Size: 15" x 6.00", "L"-type flange on Wildcat and Electra 225. Tires: LeSabre and Riviera 7.10 x 15; Wildcat 7.60 x 15, Electra 225, 8.00 x 15. Oversize tires optional on Wildcat. Whitewall tires optional on all models. **Steering:** Manual recirculating ball steering standard on LeSabre and Wildcat. Overall ratio: 33.0 to 1. Easy Power Steering standard on Electra 225 and Riviera; optional on Wildcat and LeSabre. Overall ratio: 20.7 to 1. Flexible coupling in power gear screens out vibration.

EXTERIOR DIMENSIONS:

	LeSabre	LeSabre Estate Wagons*	Wildcat	Electra 225	Riviera
Overall Length	218.93	216.76	218.93	222.84	208.10
Overall Width	78.0	78.0	78.0	78.0	76.6
Overall Height	55.7	57.9	56.4	57.5	53.2
Wheelbase	123.0	123.0	123.0	126.0	117.0
Tread—Front	62.14	62.14	62.14	62.14	60.15
Tread—Rear	61.00	61.00	61.00	61.00	59.00

*Tailgate door opening width, 54.7"; Tailgate door opening height, 29.9"; Total loading capacity, 86.6 cubic feet.

INTERIOR DIMENSIONS:

LeSABRE	Leg Room Front	Leg Room Rear	Head Room Front	Head Room Rear	Shoulder Room Front	Shoulder Room Rear
2-dr. Sport Coupe	40.9	36.0	38.3	38.1	59.0	57.7
4-dr. HardTop	40.8	37.4	38.5	33.5	58.6	57.9
4-dr. Sedan	40.8	38.7	39.3	33.8	58.6	57.9
Estate Wagons	44.5	38.1	38.3	39.7	58.8	57.9
Convertible	40.9	35.4	39.3	38.0	59.0	50.6
WILDCAT						
4-dr. Sedan	40.8	38.7	39.3	33.5	58.6	57.9
4-dr. HardTop	40.8	37.4	38.5	33.5	58.6	57.9
2-dr. Sport Coupe	40.9	36.0	38.3	38.1	59.0	57.7
Convertible	40.9	35.4	39.3	38.0	59.0	50.6
ELECTRA 225						
4-dr. Sedan	40.9	40.5	40.1	38.6	58.6	59.9
2-dr. Sport Coupe	40.5	39.2	38.5	38.4	58.6	57.5
4-dr. HardTop	40.9	38.6	38.7	38.3	58.6	58.0
4-dr. 6-window HardTop Sedan	40.9	40.5	40.1	38.6	58.6	57.9
Convertible	40.5	39.2	39.4	38.1	58.9	48.3
RIVIERA						
2-dr. Sport Coupe	40.1	35.1	37.6	37.3	56.2	55.8

Buick Motor Division, General Motors Corporation, reserves the right to make changes at any time, without notice, in prices, colors, materials, equipment, specifications and models, and also to discontinue models.

Not too noticeable, but rather surprising was the move of the Wildcat to the Electra's 126 inch wheelbase chassis. The extra 3 inches did not result in too much added weight, but there was some extra poundage.

The most noticeable change for 1965 was the marketing strategy. The Wildcat was now available in three versions. In addition to the base Wildcat, there were Deluxe and Custom versions also. A total of 10 different models were offered in the 1965 Wildcat line-up. All four body types were available in the Deluxe edition. The convertible was not offered in the base line, nor the four-door sedan in the Custom rendition.

In ascending order, Wildcat prices were: base four-door sedan, $3,182; Deluxe four-door sedan, $3,286; base 2-door Sport Coupe, $3,286; Deluxe 2-door Sport Coupe, $3,340; base four-door hardtop, $3,346; Deluxe four-door hardtop, $3,407; Deluxe convertible, $3,502; Custom two-door Sport Coupe, $3,566; Custom four-door hardtop, $3,626; and Custom convertible, $3,727.

Most popular of all these was the Custom two-door Sport Coupe, with a production total of 15,896. The two rarest models were the convertibles. There were 4,398 of the Custom made, and 4,616 of the Deluxe built. Total production of the 1965 model was 98,787—the greatest number of Wildcats for any model year. In fact, it was the third highest model year total for any high-performance passenger type Buick in history.

Standard 325 hp and optional 340 and 360 hp engines remained virtually unchanged from the previous year. Three- or 4-speed manual, or automatic transmissions were again offered, although the 3-speed could not be combined with either of the optional engines. Tom McCahill's test of the 1965 Wildcat with the 360 hp engine resulted in a 0 to 60 time of 9.1 seconds. That was slower than before, but top speed was up some to 125 mph. The "World Car Catalog" agrees with 125 for the maximum speed of the 360 hp Wildcat, while listing the 340 hp engine capable of 123 mph.

As usual, the Wildcat was included in the full-line catalogues. An additional large catalogue was issued. Entitled "the new Buick sizzlers," it included the Wildcat along with the GS versions of the Skylark and Riviera. There was also a good complement of magazine ads.

Returning after its peak year, the Wildcat was not greatly changed for 1966. The Deluxe variation was discontinued. Consequently, a convertible was added to the base series. Prices were increased so that the base Wildcats started at $3,223 for the sedan, slightly higher than the Deluxe version of a year before. The Custom models were increased too, and they ranged up to $3,701 for the convertible.

The same engines were offered, but their availability was altered slightly. The standard motor was the Wildcat 401 cubic inch V-8, with the 425 cubic inch 340 hp V-8 optional. The more potent Super Wildcat 360 hp version was still available, but in the Gran Sport option. This package included chrome plated air-cleaner, cast aluminum rocker arm covers, dual exhausts, heavy-duty front and rear suspension, positive traction differential, and GS ident plates front and rear. The Gran Sport package could be ordered only on the two-door Sport Coupe or convertible in either the base or Custom versions.

Celebrating twenty years of car testings, Tom McCahill took a Wildcat Gran Sport for the usual test spin. His 0 to 60 acceleration was just 7.5 seconds. The reason for such an improvement over the 1965 model's time he thought was due to the positive traction rear end. His top speed was a good 125 mph. The "World Car Catalog" reported 117 mph as tops for the 325 hp engine.

It is not known how many Wildcats were equipped with the Gran Sport option. The top selling models were not those on which the GS was obtainable. Most popular were the base four-door hardtop, 15,081; and the base four-door sedan, 14,389. The rarest models were the convertibles, for which the Gran Sport package was available. Production was 2,790 and 2,690 for the Deluxe and base versions respectively.

Production for the 1966 Wildcat was down over 30% from its crest the preceding year. The total was 68,584. Production was to remain in that neighborhood for the next three years.

Buick's full-line catalogue and folder included the Wildcat, as expected, but they contained surprisingly little emphasis on the Custom versions.

The full-line catalogue is excerpted in this chapter for 1965 (see pages 70-79). The full-line catalogue for 1966 is also excerpted (see pages 80-85) as well as the 1966 accessories catalogue (see pages 86-88).

THE ACCENT'S ON ACTION!

A car doesn't really come alive until you turn the key to start the engine. This is the great moment in owning a Buick. With any one of Buick's six engines and four transmissions you've bought yourself a piece of action that just won't quit. And remember that along with its reputation for performance, Buick has been steadily building a reputation for economy—three winners out of four entries in the last Mobil Economy Run—the result of steady improvement in engine design and dramatic new automatic transmission efficiency.

Here's the line-up:

FIREBALL V6—a 225 cubic inch engine that turns up 155 h.p. Smart performance. Great regular gas economy. Available on Special, Special Deluxe and Skylark. Team it with Super Turbine (optional), or regular 3-speed synchromesh transmission.

WILDCAT 445—One of the world's great performers. A 401 cubic inch V8 that scores 325 h.p. Four-barrel carburetor. Regular equipment on Wildcat, Electra 225 and Riviera. Available with Super Turbine (standard on Electra 225 and Riviera) the regular 3-speed or 4-speed synchromesh transmissions (optional on Wildcat only).

WILDCAT 310—a 300 cubic inch V8 rated a 210 h.p. Available on Special, Special Deluxe, Skylark, regular equipment on Le Sabre and Skyroof Sportwagons. Goes with Super Turbine (optional), regular 3-speed synchromesh and 4-speed synchromesh (optional) transmissions (4-speed not available for Sportwagons).

WILDCAT 465—Performance and then some! A 425 cubic inch V8 that's rated at 340 h.p. Four-barrel carburetor. Optional on Riviera, Electra 225 and Wildcat. Teamed with Super Turbine (optional on Wildcat, regular equipment on Electra 225 and Riviera) or 4-speed transmission (optional on Wildcat).

WILDCAT 355—300 cubic inches of get up and go that puts out 250 h.p. This 4-barrel V8 is available on Special, Special Deluxe, Skylark, Sportwagons and Le Sabre. Goes with Super Turbine (optional) or with the regular 3-speed or 4-speed synchromesh (optional) transmissions (4-speed not available on Le Sabre and Sportwagons).

SUPER WILDCAT—Buick's mightiest V8! Twin four-barrel carburetors and a 425 cubic inch displacement give this magnificent engine a full 360 h.p. Optional on Riviera, Electra 225, and Wildcat. Use with Super Turbine (optional on Wildcat, regular equipment on Electra 225 and Riviera) or 4-speed transmission (optional on Wildcat).

SPECIAL NOTE TO BOAT ENTHUSIASTS: Buick engines, V6 and 300 cubic inch and 401 cubic inch V8's, are now being modified for marine use by such engine manufacturers as Gray Marine, Outboard Marine, Universal Motor and Revley and are being currently used by boat makers like Sea-Ray, Matthews, Richardson and Trojan, further evidence of their outstanding durability. Consult your local boat dealer for details.

12

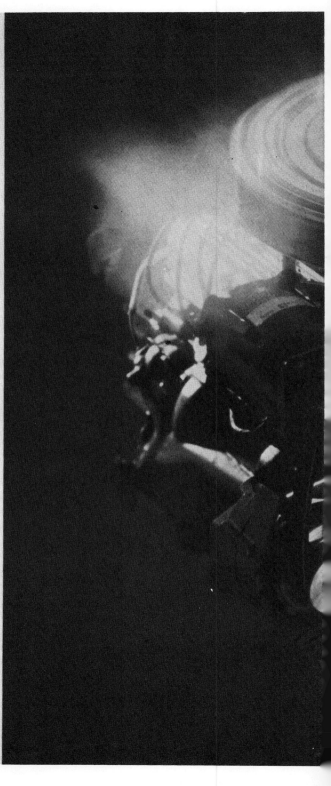

When the band down on the track strikes up "My Old Kentucky Home" to signal the beginning of still another Kentucky Derby it takes a hard-boiled cynic or a single-minded horse player to keep a dry eye. In this, the greatest of all horse-racing events, the country's leading three-year-olds compete for both money and glory. Meanwhile the city of Louisville takes on a festive air as the race brings thousands of spectators pouring into town. Not only Churchill Downs, where the race is run, but the whole city is in a state of feverish activity with parties, balls and parades—all leading up to Derby day. Our lucky girl had a ticket on Northern Dancer. Hope your horse finished in the money, too./Lady's fashions: Byck's of Louisville and St. Matthews, Kentucky.

The Buick Wildcat Sport Coupe

At the Kentucky Derby, Louisville, Kentucky | The Buick Wildcat

SOME OF THE EQUIPMENT SHOWN ON THE CARS ILLUSTRATED IS OPTIONAL AT EXTRA COST. FOR A MORE COMPLETE LISTING OF SUCH EQUIPMENT SEE PAGES 40 AND 41 OF THIS CATALOG.

Style and flair won't make a car go any faster, run any smoother or ride any softer, but it certainly does a lot for the man behind the wheel. There's a lot of pardonable satisfaction in owning a car that makes others take a second look. We think the Wildcat for 1965 is this kind of car. It's obvious that we didn't design it to blend into the landscape. It's a standout, and any red-blooded boy or girl ought to love it. But enough said about good looks; what about such items as performance, ride, handling and all-around luxury? Suffice it to say that the Wildcat excels in all departments, particularly in performance. A 401 cubic inch, 325 horsepower V8 is regular equipment, but if you're exceptionally action-minded you can choose options all the way up to 360 h.p. Enjoy the thrills of manual shifting or the smoothness of automatic Super Turbine transmission at slight extra cost. It's a real Wildcat, all right!

The Buick Wildcat Convertible

The Buick Wildcat 4-door Sedan

The Buick Wildcat 4-door Hardtop

How's this for class? It's the interior of either the Wildcat Custom Sport Coupe or Custom Convertible (optional at extra cost). Bucket seats . . . full length center console (optional with bucket seats) . . . carpeting . . . the works! By the way, if you like to track the performance of the great Wildcat engine, you can have an optional tachometer. Puts a little more zing in your driving. Also on and in the console are Super Turbine selector, storage space and smoking set. No wonder the Wildcat's wild.

SOME OF THE EQUIPMENT SHOWN ON THE CARS ILLUSTRATED IS OPTIONAL AT EXTRA COST. FOR A MORE COMPLETE LISTING OF SUCH EQUIPMENT SEE PAGES 47 AND 47 OF THIS CATALOG.

The Wildcat.
A friendly beast. Some of the time.

Wildcats come in three strengths: wild (325 bhp), wilder (340 bhp), and wildest (360 bhp).

The first one is the standard, 401-cu. in. engine. The other two bulge their muscles out to 425 cu. in.

What we've shown here is the Sport Coupe. You can also have a Wildcat as a Convertible or with four doors in Hardtop or Sedan form.

Think you can tame one?

More Wildcat Regular Equipment: *12-inch finned aluminum front brake drums; self-adjusting brakes; 8.45 x 15 tires; carpeting; padded dash; smoking set; courtesy light; map light; glove compartment light; electric wipers; crank-operated vent windows; wheel covers; dual sun visors; front seat belts.*
Some of our extra-cost options and accessories are shown on the above car.

The Wildcat 465. Extra-cost engine for the Wildcat. Horsepower—340.

The Wildcat 445. Standard engine in the Wildcat. Horsepower—325.

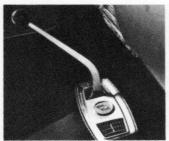

Here's what the Wildcat's console looks like, complete with shift lever for the automatic. Extra cost.

A floor-shift 4-speed is available for the Wildcat. Extra cost.

The Wildcat's tachometer. Extra cost.

One of the extra-cost interiors for the custom Wildcat Sport Coupe and Convertible.

Wildcat

Performance options: 340-bhp, 4BBL engine. 360-bhp, 2-4BBL engine. 4-speed transmission. Heavy-duty springs and shocks. Limited-slip differential. Tachometer. Chromed steel wheels.

Comfort, convenience, and appearance options: Super Turbine automatic transmission. Power steering, power brakes, power windows, power seat. Air conditioning, tinted glass. AM and AM/FM radios, electric antenna, rear seat speaker (except Conv.). Console. Windshield washers and 2-speed electric wipers. Tilting steering wheel (except with manual steering or manual transmission). Cornering lights, back-up lights, trunk light, parking brake warning light. Glare-proof mirror. Automatic trunk release. Electric clock. Remote control rear-view mirror. Whitewall tires. Rear window defroster (except Conv.).

Engines:

	Standard	Optional*	Optional*
Bhp @ rpm	325 @ 4400	340 @ 4400	360 @ 4400
Torque, lb-ft. @ rpm	445 @ 2800	465 @ 2800	465 @ 2800
Type	ohv V-8	ohv V-8	ohv V-8
Displacement, cu. in.	401	425	425
Bore and stroke	4.19 x 3.64	4.31 x 3.64	4.31 x 3.64
Carburetion	4BBL	4BBL	2-4BBL
Compression ratio	10.25:1	10.25:1	10.25:1

Short-stroke 90° V-8, cast iron alloy block, with five main bearings. Intake valves —1.875". Exhaust valves—1.50". Low-restriction dual exhausts standard on 360-bhp engine, optional on others.

*Not available with 3-speed manual transmission.

Transmissions: The standard transmission is a 3-speed, its shift lever mounted on the steering column. Ratios are 2.49, 1.59, and 1.00:1. A close-ratio 4-speed is available, its shift lever mounted on the floor. Ratios are 2.20, 1.64, 1.31, and 1.00:1. Also available is a 3-speed torque convertor automatic with a column shift —or, at extra cost, with its shift lever mounted in a console. Ratios are 2.48, 1.48, and 1.00:1, with a total torque multiplication of 5.50:1.

Axle ratios:

Engine	Transmission	Standard Axle Ratio	Special Order Axle Ratios			
325 bhp	3- or 4-speed	3.42	3.23	3.58	3.91	
	Automatic	3.07	2.78	3.36	3.42	3.58
340 and	4-speed	3.42	3.23	3.58	3.91	
360 bhp	Automatic	3.07	2.78	3.36	3.42	3.58

Suspension: Ball joint independent front, four-link rear. Coil springs, front and rear. Heavy-duty springs and shocks are available on special order.

Steering: Recirculating ball bearing steering gear. Manual ratio—28:1. Power steering ratio—17.5:1.

Brakes: Hydraulic, duo-servo, internal expanding, self-adjusting. Drums are 12" finned aluminum, front; 12" finned cast iron, rear. Swept area —320.5 sq. in.

Dimensions and capacities: Wheelbase is 126 inches. Tread is 63.4 inches front, 63 inches rear. Overall length is 219.8 inches. Overall width is 80 inches. Height is 55.2 inches. The gas tank holds approximately 25 gallons.

**The 1966 Wildcat.
We checked out its tuning by driving it up and
down steep mountain roads.**

We tested the new Wildcat
very, very thoroughly.
For instance, we drove down
steep mountain sides; we tested
the brakes, the engine, the body mounts,
the frame, the suspension.
The result? We give you a Wildcat
for '66 that's tuned like a Swiss watch
—every part works with every
other part. On pavement, on dirt,
on gravel, up hills and down hills,
you'll never drive a tougher car
—nor a more comfortable one.

Wildcat has a smart new grille
this year. The front and rear
views have been re-designed
as well. Beautiful.
Even the instrument panel
inside is new.

Remember the mountain road bit?
After that, we worked on
Wildcat's suspension.
And the frame.
And the springs.
And the stabilizer.
We came up with a
comfortable,
but firm, ride.

In spite of the agile look,
Wildcat is a big car—
a family car.
Take the wheelbase, for instance.
It's 126 inches long. That gives you
more family room inside.
You could even pack in a tall dog.
There's over 37 inches
of head room in the rear.

(Wheel covers illustrated are a dealer installed accessory.)

We've got a new standard automatic transmission for the Wildcat this year. The Super Turbine— smooth, responsive power.

Pampering equipment. We've made available a whole closet-full of convenience features. Power steering, power brakes, AM-FM radio, bucket seats, reclining front passenger seat with head rests— the list goes on. Big car luxury never had it so complete.

Wildcat's standard engine this year is a 325-horsepower V8. More? Our 340-horsepower V8 is available.

There are four Wildcat models for 1966. A sport coupe, a 4-door hardtop, a 4-door sedan, and a convertible.

Have a ball at your Buick dealer's driving the 1966 Buick.

(Some of the equipment shown on the car illustrated is optional at extra cost.)

The Wildcat Sport Coupe

The Wildcat 4-Door Sedan

(Some of the equipment shown on the car illustrated is optional at extra cost.)

10

The seat on the left, with the handy centre pull down armrest, is regular equipment in the Wildcat 4-door sedan and optional at extra cost on the 4-door hardtop. All-vinyl bucket seats as you see on the right are available in the Wildcat sport coupe and convertible. Let them caress you when you pay a visit to your Buick dealer.

Notch-Back vinyl bench seats are are also available in the Wildcat sport coupe, 4-door hardtop and convertible.

Seat colors available are blue in all models. Black in all models except 4-door sedan. A fawn interior is available in the sport coupe and turquoise, fawn, green and slate are available in the 4-door hardtop sedan. You can also get green and slate in the 4-door sedan. If you want a red interior, buy a convertible.

**The Wildcat lounge:
Comfort like this makes you wonder if a Wildcat isn't something more than just an automobile.**

Seat belts are also regular equipment for both front and back. Retractors for the front seat are optional at extra cost. Release the belt and it scoots out of sight.

Wildcat bucket seats that recline on the passenger side are available. And you can get head rests for all seats.

Study these pages and you'll become a Wildcat expert. Nice hobby.

The Wildcat 4-Door Hardtop

The Wildcat Convertible

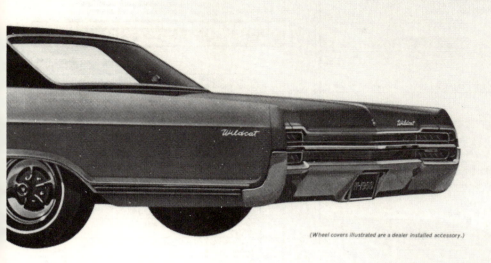

(Some of the equipment shown on the cars illustrated is optional at extra cost from dealer or factory.)

(Wheel covers illustrated are a dealer installed accessory.)

BUICK WILDCAT REGULAR EQUIPMENT—325-hp. Wildcat 445 V8; 3-speed Super Turbine Automatic Transmission. Heater and Defroster; Finned Aluminum Front Brake Drums; Seat Belts—Front and Rear; Step-On Parking Brake; Directional Signals; Front Door-operated Courtesy Light; Glove Compartment Light; Smoking Set; Rear Seat Ash Trays; Magic-Mirror Finish; Dual Arm Rests—Front and Rear; 15-inch Wheels; Dual Horns; Crank-operated Vent Windows; Delcotron Generator; Self-Adjusting Brakes; Carpeting; Dual-Key Locking System; Re-usable Air Cleaner Element; Full-Flow Oil Filter; Plunger-type Door Locks; Custom Interior Trims; Deluxe Steering Wheel; Paddle-type Arm Rest; Custom Headlining; Cross-Flow Radiator; Upper Instrument Panel Pad; Outside Rear View Mirror; Dual Speed Windshield Wiper with glare resistant arms and blades and Windshield Washer; Padded Sun Visors; Back-up Lamps.

THE STANDARD ENGINE. WILDCAT 445

Horsepower	Torque	Compression Ratio	Displacement	Carburetion	Fuel
325 @ 4400	445 @ 2800	10.25 to 1	401	4-barrel	Premium

THE OPTIONAL ENGINE. WILDCAT 465

Horsepower	Torque	Compression Ratio	Displacement	Carburetion	Fue.
340 @ 4400	465 @ 2800	10.25 to 1	425	4-barrel	Premium

THE INCREDIBLE TRANSMISSION
Regular Equipment
Super Turbine

REAR AXLE RATIOS.

	Super Turbine
	3.07

EXTERIOR DIMENSIONS. (Approximations in inches.)

	Length	Width	Height	Wheelbase	Tread-Front	Tread-Rear
Sport Coupe	219.9	80.0	56.1	126.0	63.4	63.0
4-Door Hardtop	219.9	80.0	56.0	126.0	63.4	63.0
4-Door Sedan	219.9	80.0	55.9	126.0	63.4	63.0
Convertible	219.9	80.0	55.9	126.0	63.4	63.0

INTERIOR DIMENSIONS. (More Approximations in inches.)

	Head Room Front	Rear	Leg Room Front	Rear	Shoulder Room Front	Rear
Sport Coupe	38.3	37.2	42.4	34.9	62.2	61.0
4-Door Hardtop	38.1	37.3	42.2	38.5	62.3	61.4
4-Door Sedan	38.9	37.7	42.2	39.0	62.3	61.4
Convertible	39.0	37.8	42.4	34.9	62.2	53.1

SOME GOOD READING:

Engine Lubricating System: Main bearings, connecting rods and camshaft bearings pressure lubricated. Cylinder walls splash and nozzle lubricated. Normal oil pressure 40 @ 2400. Full-flow oil filter. Crankcase capacity (refills less filter) 3½ quarts. **Fuel System:** Automatic choke. Mechanical fuel pump. Two-stage gasoline filter with fine filter in fuel tank. Oil impregnated polyurethane air cleaner. Exhaust type intake manifold heat control. Fuel Tank Capacity: approximately 20.8 gallons. **Engine Cooling:** Pressure system. Choke-type circulation thermostat. Capacity: 14.0 quarts with heater. **Exhaust System:** Muffler constructed of corrosion resistant aluminized steel. Dual exhaust available as optional equipment. **Electrical:** Twelve volt electrical system. Four position starter-ignition switch. **Automatic Transmission:** Super Turbine is a torque converter type featuring a variable pitch stator within the converter; and two planetary gear sets. Total oil capacity 18.0 pints. **Propeller Shaft:** Drive shaft is slightly angled to reduce tunnel height in rear seat. Angled sections are connected by a special constant-velocity universal joint that minimizes vibration during transfer of power to rear axle. Shaft is connected to transmission and rear axle by needle bearing universal joints. **Rear Axle:** Hypoid gears, semi-floating. Transfer of driving forces through rubber-mounted arms connected to frame. **Frame:** Perimeter-type. **Suspension:** Independent ball-joint front suspension with link-type stabilizer bar. Four-link-type rear suspension. Coil springs front and rear. Direct acting hydraulic shock absorbers front and rear. **Brakes:** Hydraulic, self-energizing. Air-cooled finned aluminum brake drums front; finned drums rear. Total gross lining area; 197.32 sq. in. Step-on parking brake operating through rear service brake shoes. Power brakes optional at extra cost. **Steering:** Manual recirculating ball steering standard. Overall ratio: 33.4 to 1. Easy Power Steering, optional. Overall ratio: 19.5 to 1. Flexible coupling in power gear screens out vibration.

'66 WILDCAT SPECIFICATIONS

Standard Engine

	Horsepower	Torque	Compression Ratio	Displacement	Carburetion	Fuel
WILDCAT 445	325 @ 4400	445 @ 2800	10.25 to 1	401	4-barrel	Premium

Optional Engine

	Horsepower	Torque	Compression Ratio	Displacement	Carburetion	Fuel
WILDCAT 465	340 @ 4400	465 @ 2800	10.25 to 1	425	4-barrel	Premium

Transmissions

Regular Equipment	3-Speed Manual	Option (Automatic) Super Turbine

Rear Axle Ratios
(Optional Rear Axle Ratios available.)

	3-Speed Manual Trans. Standard		Super Turbine Standard	
WILDCAT 445 V-8	—	3.23	—	3.07
WILDCAT 465 V-8	N.A. with 3-Speed Manual Trans.		—	3.07
WITH GRAN SPORT OPTION	N.A. with 3-Speed Manual Trans.		—	3.23

Exterior Dimensions (In inches)

	Length	Width	Height	Wheelbase	Tread-Front	Tread-Rear
Sport Coupe	219.9	80.0	54.5	126.0	63.4	63.0
4-door Hardtop	220.1	80.0	54.4	126.0	63.4	63.0
4-door Sedan	220.1	80.0	55.4	126.0	63.4	63.0
Convertible	220.1	80.0	54.3	126.0	63.4	63.0

Interior Dimensions (In inches)

	Head Room Front	Rear	Leg Room Front	Rear	Shoulder Room Front	Rear
Sport Coupe	38.3	37.2	42.4	34.9	62.2	61.0
4-door Hardtop	38.1	37.3	42.2	38.5	62.3	61.4
4-door Sedan	38.9	37.7	42.2	39.0	62.3	61.4
Convertible	39.0	37.8	42.4	34.9	62.2	53.1

WILDCAT OPTIONS

OPERATION AND PERFORMANCE

Code		Mfr's.* Suggested Retail Price
A7	340-hp. Wildcat 465 V-8 Engine (425 cu. in., 4-bbl. Carburetor)	$47.37
A9	Wildcat Gran Sport High Performance Group (Includes 340-hp. Wildcat 465 V-8 Engine with chrome-plated air cleaner and cast aluminum rocker arm covers, dual exhaust, heavy-duty suspension, Positive Traction Differential, 8.45 x 15 Whitewall Tires, and Gran Sport identifying ornamentation. Available with C5 or C6)	$254.71
B2	Super Turbine Transmission	$236.82
B4	Operating Console (Available only with Super Turbine and Bucket Seats on Custom Sport Coupe and Convertible)	$47.37
C5	Power Steering with 15:1 Steering Ratio (Available with A9 on Sport Coupes and Convertible)	$121.04
C6	Power Steering (Required with 3-speed Manual Transmission)	$105.25
C7	Power Brakes (Not available with 3-speed Manual Transmission)	$42.10
D1	Sonomatic Radio with Manual Antenna	$88.41
D2	Sonomatic Radio with Electric Antenna	$113.98
D4	AM-FM Stereo Radio with Speakers front and rear, plus Electric Antenna	$266.81
D5	AM-FM Radio with Electric Antenna	$175.24
D6	Rear Seat Speaker (Included with D4)	$16.84
E1	Dual Exhaust (Not available with 3-speed Manual Transmission)	$30.53
E2	Closed Crankcase Ventilation (Calif. only) (Required in combination with E6)	$5.27
E6	Air Injection Reactor (Calif. only) (Required in combination with E2)	$44.73
F1	Whitewall Tires (8.45 x 15—2-ply with 4-ply rating. Standard with A9)	$42.41
F2	Whitewall Tires (8.85 x 15—2-ply with 4-ply rating) Wildcat / Wildcat with A9	$69.26 / $21.05
F3	Blackwall Tires (8.85 x 15—2-ply with 4-ply rating) (Not available with A9)	$22.31
F8	Red Line Tires (8.45 x 15—2-ply with 4-ply rating) With A9 only	No Charge
G1	Performance Axle with Positive Traction Differential Wildcat without A9 / Wildcat with A9	$47.37 / No Charge

AND ACCESSORIES

Code		Mfr's.* Suggested Retail Price
G4	Positive Traction Differential (Included with G1 and standard with A9)	$47.37
G5	Economy Axle	No Charge
H1	Trailer Spring Option (Rear Springs only)	$3.79
H2	Heavy-duty Suspension (Includes Rear Springs, Front and Rear Shocks)	$3.79
I6	Air Conditioner (Not available with I8 or 3-speed Manual Transmission)	$421.00
I7	Air Conditioner Modification (Not available with 3-speed Manual Transmission)	$21.05
I8	Less Heater and Defroster	($95.90)

COMFORT AND CONVENIENCE

Code		Mfr's.* Suggested Retail Price
J1	Custom Seat Belts—2 retractable front belts plus 2 rear belts	$10.53
K1	Safety Group (Glare-reducing Mirror, Parking Brake Signal Light, Safety Buzzer and Courtesy Lights. Safety Buzzer is not available with S6)	$23.16
K2	Cornering Lights (Not available with 3-speed Manual Transmission)	$33.68
L1	Soft-Ray Tinted Glass (All windows)	$42.10
L2	Soft-Ray Tinted Glass (Windshield only)	$28.42
M7	Rear Window Defroster (Not available on Convertible)	$21.05
N2	Four-Note Horn	$15.79
O4	Door Guards—2-door	$4.74
O4	Door Guards—4-door	$8.16
O5	Remote Control Outside Rear View Mirror	$7.20
P1	Carpet Savers and Handy Mats	$12.19
P2	Carpet Savers	$6.77
Q4	Power Seat—6-way (Bench Seat)	$94.73
Q5	Power Seat—4-way Tilt Adjuster (Bench or Bucket Seat)	$69.47
Q6	Custom-padded Cushions (Standard on Wildcat Custom)	$22.11
R1	Power Windows	$105.25
S6	Electro-Cruise Control (Not available with 3-speed Manual Transmission) Not available with K1 Available with K1	$63.15 $55.79
S7	Tilt Steering Wheel (Not available with 3-speed Manual Transmission or manual steering)	$42.10

Code		Mfr's.* Suggested Retail Price
T1	Automatic Trunk Release	$12.63
T2	Vacuum-operated Door Locks—2-door	$44.73
T2	Vacuum-operated Door Locks—4-door	$68.42
U4	Accessory Group (Electric Clock, License Plate Frame, and Trunk Light)	$21.05
U5	Tachometer (B4 must be specified) (Custom Sport Coupe and Custom Convertible)	$47.37

APPEARANCE OPTIONS

Code		Mfr's.* Suggested Retail Price
V2	Chrome-plated Wheels	$89.47
V3	Wire Wheel Covers	$57.89
W6	Custom Bright Exterior Moldings (Belt Reveal and Door Window Frames) (4-door Sedan only)	$38.95
X1	Custom Steering Wheel	$52.63
1B	Reclining Passenger Seat with Headrests for both driver and passenger—Bucket Seats (Sport Coupes and Convertibles only)	$84.20
1C	Headrests for Bench Seats (Driver and Passenger)	$42.10
1D	Headrests for Bucket Seats (Driver and Passenger) (Sport Coupes and Convertibles only)	$52.63
**	Custom Trim Strato-Bucket Seats—Vinyl (Regular Sport Coupe and Convertible only)	$115.78
**	Custom Vinyl Top (Sport Coupes and 4-door Hardtops only)	$110.52
**	Two-Tone Paint (Includes Rear Quarter Belt Reveal Molding)	$26.32
**	Special Order Paint (Other than standard color—single car order)	$84.20

WILDCAT/TUNED FOR SUPER ACTION

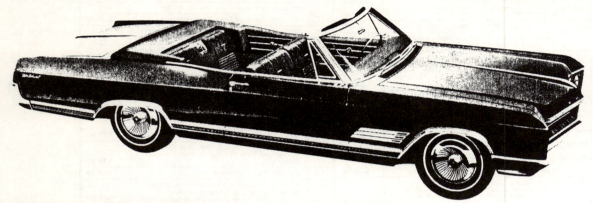

MODELS AND PRICES

MODEL	BODY STYLE	PRICE*
6437	Sport Coupe	$3,326.00
6439	4-door Hardtop	3,391.00
6467	Convertible	3,480.00
6469	4-door Sedan	3,233.00
6637	Custom Sport Coupe	3,547.00
6639	Custom 4-door Hardtop	3,606.00
6667	Custom Convertible	3,701.00

REGULAR EQUIPMENT

- 325-hp. Wildcat 445 V-8
- 3-speed Manual Transmission (Synchronized in all forward gears)
- Heater and Defroster
- Finned Aluminum Front Brake Drums
- Step-On Parking Brake
- Directional Signals
- Front Door-operated Courtesy Light
- Glove Compartment Light
- Smoking Set
- Rear Seat Ash Trays
- Magic-Mirror Finish
- Dual Arm Rests—front and rear

- 15-inch Wheels
- Dual Horns
- Crank-operated Vent Windows
- 6,000-mile Lubed Front Suspension
- Delcotron Generator
- Wildcat Wheel Covers
- Self-adjusting Brakes
- Carpeting
- Dual-Key Locking System
- Re-usable Air Cleaner Element
- Full-flow Oil Filter
- Plunger-type Door Locks
- Custom Interior Trims (Wildcat Custom Models)
- Deluxe Steering Wheel (Wildcat Custom Models)
- Paddle-type Arm Rest (Wildcat Custom Models)
- Custom Headlining (Wildcat Custom Models—except Convertible)
- Cross-flow Radiator
- Back-up Lights
- Electric Dual-speed Windshield Wipers
- Windshield Washer
- Outside Rear View Mirror
- Padded Upper Instrument Panel
- Dual Padded Sun Visors
- Seat Belts—front and rear

*Manufacturer's Suggested Retail Prices shown include Federal Excise Tax and suggested dealer delivery and handling charge, but do not include destination charges, optional equipment and accessories, license fees, or state and local taxes.
All prices, specifications, etc., are subject to change without notice.

The same body types in the same subseries were offered in the modestly revised 1967 Wildcat. Prices were up $40 or $50 to a range of $3,277 for the base 4-door sedan to $3,757 for the Custom convertible. There was no Gran Sport option this year.

Only one engine was available. Also used in the Electra and Riviera, this new engine, displacing 430 cubic inches, developed 360 hp. The only transmission available was the Super Turbine automatic. However, the buyer did have a choice of column- or console-mounted shifting. According to the "World Car Catalog," top speed was 120 mph.

The base four-door hardtop continued to be the Wildcat's best seller at 15,110 copies, with the four-door sedan a close second at 14,579. And the convertibles continued to be the rarest. There were 2,276 made in the base version and 2,913 with Custom trim. The model year's total production was up slightly to 70,881 units.

Very little information about the performance of the 1967 Wildcat is to be found. Other Buick models were receiving the attention of the performance press.

Two large all-model Buick catalogues, one a deluxe edition and the other a cheaper version, as well as a small all-model folder covered the Wildcat series. There was no exclusive Wildcat brochure for 1967.

The major restyling to the familiar Wildcat grille did not signify other extensive changes for the 1968 models. Just minor facelifting was applied elsewhere to the Wildcat.

The convertible of the base subseries was deleted from the line-up. Prices rose $116 on the surviving Custom convertible, and $139 on all other models. The price range was now from $3,416 to $3,873.

As usual, the four-door hardtop was the model year's most popular model, with the four-door sedan almost as popular. Production was 15,201 and 15,153, respectively. The rarest model, not surprisingly, was the convertible, with a 3,572 total. Total Wildcat production for the model year was 69,969, which was down about 900 units from a year earlier.

The 430 cubic inch V-8 motor continued to spew out 360 hp. Again, it was the only engine obtainable in a Wildcat. The automatic transmission, with a choice of control locations, was also continued from 1967, but it was an option. The standard transmission was a 3-speed column mounted manual gear box. Again the top speed was reported by the "World Car Catalog" to be 120 mph.

Just one full-line Buick catalogue was issued for the year. It covered the Wildcat in its 74 pages. A full-line folder was also published.

The literature excerpted in this chapter includes the full-line showroom catalogues for 1967 and 1968 (see pages 90-95 and 96-103, respectively).

Spring was never like this . . . Wildcat

The Wildcat & Wilhelmina

"I know cars quite well.
I know what they should be
and what they are.
Buick is a very good car;
it is strong, but quiet.
I can sense its strength and power.
"But what makes Buick
one of the world's best automobiles
is that it is a complete automobile.
It has power, yes.
But it is also luxurious.
It is sporty.
It is elegant.
It is tailored.
"I think American automobiles
have undergone
the same kind of change as fashions
in the last ten years.
They've become very young.
But too often they're showy.
Perhaps this is why
I've always appreciated Buick.
It is very modern.
But it is also very elegant.
When I saw this Wildcat,
I fell madly in love with it."

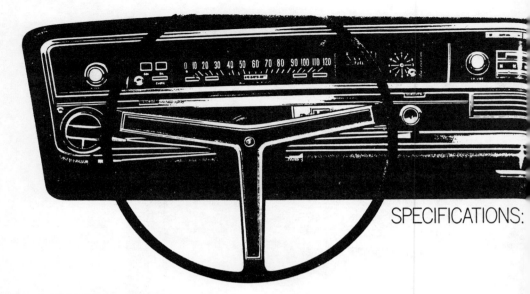

SPECIFICATIONS:

BUICK RIVIERA REGULAR EQUIPMENT—SuperTurbine Transmission; 360-hp. 430-4 V-8; Power Steering; Self-adjusting Power Brakes; Tilt Steering Wheel; Dual Exhausts; Heater and Defroster; Finned Aluminum Front Brake Drums; Custom Padded Seat Cushions; Custom Front Seat Belts with Retractors; Rear Seat Belts; Electric Clock; Step-On Parking Brake; Parking Brake Signal Light; Directional Signals; Trunk Light; Door-operated Courtesy Lights; Glove Compartment Light; Glareproof Mirror; Smoking Set; Rear Seat Ash Trays; Magic-Mirror Finish; Dual Arm Rests—Front and Rear; 15-inch Wheels; Wheel Covers; Dual Horns; License Plate Frames; 6,000-mile Lubed Front Suspension; Delcotron Generator; Carpeting; Dual-Key Locking System; Re-usable Air Cleaner Element; Full-Flow Oil Filter; Plunger-type Door Locks; Upper Instrument Panel Pad; Outside Rear View Mirror; Dual Speed Windshield Wiper and Windshield Washer; Padded Sun Visors; Back-up Lamps.
NOTE: All Buick models feature the basic safety equipment listed on pages 12 and 13 as standard.

THE STANDARD ENGINE: 430-4

Horsepower	Torque	Compression Ratio	Displacement	Carburetion	Fuel
360 @ 5000	475 @ 3200	10.25 to 1	430	4-barrel	Premium

THE TRANSMISSIONS:

Regular Equipment	Option
Automatic SuperTurbine (Column Shift)	Automatic SuperTurbine (Console Shift)

REAR AXLE RATIOS:

Riviera	3.07
Riviera GS	3.42

EXTERIOR DIMENSIONS: (Approximations in inches.)

Length	Width	Height	Wheelbase	Tread-front	Tread-rear
211.3	79.4	53.2	119.0	63.5	63.0

INTERIOR DIMENSIONS: (Approximations in inches.)

Head Room		Leg Room		Shoulder Room	
Front	Rear	Front	Rear	Front	Rear
41.2	37.4	41.2	36.6	58.7	56.4

THE OPTIONAL RIVIERA GRAN SPORT. Suspension, both front and rear, is heavy duty. Positive traction differential (3.42 axle ratio standard). Monogram—front fender "GS". Monogram—instrument panel "Riviera GS", H70-15 (8.75 x 15) wide oval type tires with white stripe are standard. Red stripe tires are available at no extra cost.

SOME GOOD READING: **Engine Lubricating System:** Main bearings, connecting rods and camshaft bearings pressure lubricated. Cylinder walls splash and nozzle lubricated. Normal oil pressure 30 @ 2800. Full-flow oil filter. Crankcase capacity (refill less filter) 4 quarts. **Fuel System:** Automatic choke. Mechanical fuel pump. Two-stage gasoline filter with fine filter in fuel tank. Oil impregnated polyurethane air cleaner. Exhaust type manifold heat control. Fuel Tank Capacity: approximately 21 gallons. **Engine Cooling:** Pressure system. Choke-type circulation thermostat. Centrifugal water pump. Capacity: 18.5 quarts with heater. **Exhaust System:** Muffler constructed of corrosion resistant aluminized stainless steel to promote longer life. Dual exhaust. **Electrical:** Twelve volt electrical system. Four-position starter-ignition switch. **Automatic Transmission:** SuperTurbine is a torque converter type featuring a variable pitch stator within the converter; and two single planetary gear sets. Total oil capacity: 22 pints. **Propeller Shaft:** Drive shaft is slightly angled to reduce tunnel height in rear seat. Angled sections are connected by a special constant-velocity universal joint that minimizes vibration during transfer of power to rear axle. Shaft is connected to transmission and rear axle by needle-bearing universal joints. **Rear axle:** Hypoid gears, semi-floating. **Frame:** Cruciform. **Suspension:** Independent ball-joint front suspension with link type stabilizer bar. Four-link-type rear suspension. Coil springs front and rear. Direct acting hydraulic shock absorbers front and rear. **Brakes:** Gross lining area 193.3 sq. in. Step-on parking brake operating through rear service brake shoes. Power brakes standard. **Tires:** 8.45 x 15. **Steering:** Easy power steering standard. Overall ratio: 19.0 to 1. Flexible coupling in power gear screens out road irregularities.

BUICK ELECTRA 225 REGULAR EQUIPMENT—SuperTurbine Transmission 360-hp. 430-4 V-8; Power Steering; Self-adjusting Power Brakes; Custom Padded Seat Cushions; Custom Front Seat Belts with Retractors; Rear Seat Belts; Electric Clock; Step-On Parking Brake; Parking Brake Signal Light; Deluxe Steering Wheel; Directional Signals; Trunk Light; Door-operated Courtesy Light; Glove Compartment Light; Smoking Set; Rear Seat Ash Trays; Glareproof Mirror; Magic-Mirror Finish; Dual Side Arm Rests—Front and Rear; 15-inch Wheels; Deluxe Wheel Covers; Dual Horns; License Plate Frames; 6,000 mile Lubed Front Suspension; Delcotron Generator; Carpeting on Floors and Doors; Dual-Key Locking System; Re-usable Air Cleaner Element; Full-Flow Oil Filter; Plunger-type Door Locks; Custom Interior Trims (Electra 225 Custom Models); Cross-Flow Radiator; Upper Instrument Panel Pad; Outside Rear View Mirror; Dual Speed Windshield Wiper and Windshield Washer; Padded Sun Visors; Back-up Lamps.
NOTE: All Buick models feature the basic safety equipment listed on pages 12 and 13 as standard.

THE STANDARD ENGINE: 430-4

Horsepower	Torque	Compression Ratio	Displacement	Carburetion	Fuel
360 @ 5000	475 @ 3200	10.25 to 1	430	4-barrel	Premium

THE TRANSMISSIONS:

Regular Equipment

REAR AXLE RATIOS:
SuperTurbine 2.78

EXTERIOR DIMENSIONS: (Approximations in inches.)

	Length	Width	Height	Wheelbase	Tread-front	Tread-rear
Sport Coupe	223.9	80.0	55.0	126.0	63.4	63.0
4-Door Hardtop	223.9	80.0	55.0	126.0	63.4	63.0
4-Door Sedan	223.9	80.0	56.2	126.0	63.4	63.0
Convertible	223.9	80.0	55.0	126.0	63.4	63.0

INTERIOR DIMENSIONS: (Approximations in inches.)

	Head Room		Leg Room		Shoulder Room	
	Front	Rear	Front	Rear	Front	Rear
Sport Coupe	38.5	37.9	41.7	38.3	62.2	60.7
4-Door Hardtop	38.6	37.7	42.2	38.9	62.2	61.2
4-Door Sedan	39.5	38.2	42.2	42.1	62.2	61.0
Convertible	38.8	37.8	41.7	41.7	62.1	52.5

SOME GOOD READING: **Engine Lubricating System:** Main bearings, connecting rods and camshaft bearings pressure lubricated. Cylinder walls splash and nozzle lubricated. Normal oil pressure 30 @ 2800. Full-flow oil filter. Crankcase capacity (refill less filter) 4 quarts. **Fuel System:** Automatic choke. Mechanical fuel pump. Two-stage gasoline filter in fuel tank. Oil impregnated polyurethane air cleaner. Exhaust type intake manifold heat control. **Fuel Tank Capacity:** approximately 25 gallons. **Engine Cooling:** Pressure system. Choke-type circulation thermostat. Centrifugal water pump. **Capacity:** 18.5 quarts with heater. **Exhaust System:** Muffler constructed of corrosion resistant aluminized steel to promote longer life. Dual exhaust available as optional equipment. **Electrical:** Twelve volt electrical system. Four-position starter-ignition switch. **Automatic Transmission:** SuperTurbine is a torque converter type featuring a variable pitch stator within the converter; and two planetary gear sets. Total oil capacity refill 22 pints. **Propeller Shaft:** Drive shaft is slightly angled to reduce tunnel height in rear seat. Angled sections are connected by a special constant-velocity universal joint that minimizes vibration during transfer of power to rear axle. Shaft is connected to transmission and rear axle by needle-bearing universal joints. **Rear Axle:** Hypoid gears, semi-floating. Transfer of driving forces through rubber-mounted arms connected to frame. **Frame:** Perimeter-type. **Suspension:** Independent ball-joint front suspension with link-type stabilizer bar. Four-link-type rear suspension. Coil springs front and rear. Direct acting hydraulic shock absorbers front and rear. **Brakes:** Hydraulic self-energizing. Air-cooled finned aluminum brake drums front; finned drums rear. Total gross lining area 193.3 sq. in. Step-on parking brake operating through rear service brake shoes. Power brakes standard. **Tires:** 8.85 x 15. **Steering:** Easy Power Steering standard. Overall ratio: 19.5 to 1. Flexible coupling in power gear screens out road irregularities.

BUICK WILDCAT REGULAR EQUIPMENT—SuperTurbine Transmission 360-hp. 430-4 V-8; Heater and Defroster; Finned Aluminum Front Brake Drums; Seat Belts—Front and Rear; Step-On Parking Brake; Directional Signals; Front Door-operated Courtesy Light; Glove Compartment Light; Smoking Set; Rear Seat Ash Trays; Magic-Mirror Finish; Dual Side Arm Rests—Front and Rear; 15-inch Wheels; Dual Horns; Crank-operated Vent Windows; 6,000-mile Lubed Front Suspension; Delcotron Generator; Self-Adjusting Brakes; Carpeting; Dual-Key Locking System; Re-usable Air Cleaner Element; Full-Flow Oil Filter; Plunger-type Door Locks; Custom Interior Trims (Wildcat Custom Models); Deluxe Steering Wheel; Paddle-type Arm Rest (Wildcat Custom Models); Custom Headlining (Wildcat Custom Models—except Convertible); Cross-Flow Radiator; Upper Instrument Panel Pad; Outside Rear View Mirror; Dual Speed Windshield Wiper and Windshield Washer; Padded Sun Visors; Back-up Lamps.
NOTE: All Buick models feature the basic safety equipment listed on pages 12 and 13 as standard.

THE STANDARD ENGINE: 430-4

Horsepower	Torque	Compression Ratio	Displacement	Carburetion	Fuel
360 @ 5000	475 @ 3200	10.25 to 1	430	4-barrel	Premium

THE TRANSMISSIONS:

Regular Equipment	Option
Automatic SuperTurbine (Column Shift)	Automatic SuperTurbine (Console Shift)

REAR AXLE RATIOS:
SuperTurbine 3.07

EXTERIOR DIMENSIONS: (Approximations in inches.)

	Length	Width	Height	Wheelbase	Tread-front	Tread-rear
Sport Coupe	220.5	80.0	54.9	126.0	63.4	63.0
4-Door Hardtop	220.5	80.0	54.8	126.0	63.4	63.0
4-Door Sedan	220.5	80.0	55.7	126.0	63.4	63.0
Convertible	220.5	80.0	54.8	126.0	63.4	63.0

Riviera, Electra 225, Wildcat, LeSabre and Sportwagon.

INTERIOR DIMENSIONS: (Approximations in inches.)

	Head Room		Leg Room		Shoulder Room	
	Front	Rear	Front	Rear	Front	Rear
Sport Coupe	38.4	37.2	42.3	34.9	62.2	62.2
4-Door Hardtop	38.1	37.3	42.3	38.5	62.3	62.3
4-Door Sedan	38.9	37.7	42.2	39.0	62.3	62.3
Convertible	39.0	37.9	42.3	34.9	62.2	62.2

SOME GOOD READING: Engine Lubricating System: Main bearings, connecting rods and camshaft bearings pressure lubricated. Cylinder walls splash and nozzle lubricated. Normal oil pressure 30 @ 2800. Full-flow oil filter. Crankcase capacity (refill less filter) 4 quarts. **Fuel System:** Automatic choke. Mechanical fuel pump. Two-stage gasoline filter with fine filter in fuel tank. Oil impregnated polyurethane air cleaner. Exhaust type intake manifold heat control. Fuel Tank Capacity: approximately 25 gallons. **Engine Cooling:** Pressure system. Choke-type circulation thermostat. Capacity: 18.5 quarts with heater. **Exhaust System:** Muffler constructed of corrosion resistant aluminized steel to promote longer life. Dual exhaust available as optional equipment. **Electrical:** Twelve volt electrical system. Four position starter-ignition switch. **Automatic Transmission:** SuperTurbine is a torque converter type featuring a variable pitch stator within the converter; and two planetary gear sets. Total oil capacity 22 pints. **Propeller Shaft:** Drive shaft is slightly angled to reduce tunnel height in rear seat. Angled sections are connected by a special constant-velocity universal joint that minimizes vibration during transfer of power to rear axle. Shaft is connected to transmission and rear axle by needle-bearing universal joints. **Rear Axle:** Hypoid gears, semi-floating. Transfer of driving forces through rubber-mounted arms connected to frame. **Frame:** Perimeter-type. **Suspension:** Independent ball-joint front suspension with link-type stabilizer bar. Four-link-type rear suspension. Coil springs front and rear. Direct acting hydraulic shock absorbers front and rear. **Brakes:** Hydraulic, self-energizing. Air-cooled finned aluminum brake drums front. Finned drums rear. Total gross lining area 193.3 sq. in. Step-on parking brake operating through rear service brake shoes. Power brakes optional. **Tires:** 8.45 x 15. Optional tires available for other than normal driving conditions. Consult your Buick dealer. **Steering:** Easy Power Steering, Std. Overall ratio 19.5 to 1. Flexible coupling in power gear screens out road irregularities.

BUICK LeSABRE REGULAR EQUIPMENT—220-hp. 340-2 V-8; 3-speed Manual Transmission (synchronized in all forward gears); Heater and Defroster; Finned Alloy Brake Drums; Seat Belts—Front and Rear; Step-On Parking Brake; Directional Signals; Front Door-operated Courtesy Light; Glove Compartment Light; Smoking Set; Rear Seat Ash Trays; Magic-Mirror Finish; Dual Side Arm Rests—Front and Rear; 15-inch Wheels; Dual Horns; Crank-operated Vent Windows; 6,000-mile Lubed Front Suspension; Delcotron Generator; Self-adjusting Brakes; Carpeting; Dual-Key Locking System; Re-usable Air Cleaner Element; Full-Flow Oil Filter; Plunger-type Door Locks; Custom Interior Trims (LeSabre Custom Models); Deluxe Steering Wheel; Cross-Flow Radiator; Upper Instrument Panel Pad; Outside Rear View Mirror; Dual Speed Windshield Wiper and Windshield Washer; Padded Sun Visors; Back-up Lamps.
NOTE: All Buick models feature the basic safety equipment listed on pages 12 and 13 as standard.

THE STANDARD ENGINE: 340-2

Horsepower	Torque	Compression Ratio	Displacement	Carburetion	Fuel
220 @ 4200	340 @ 2400	9.0 to 1	340	2-barrel	Regular

THE OPTIONAL ENGINE: 340-4

Horsepower	Torque	Compression Ratio	Displacement	Carburetion	Fuel
260 @ 4200	365 @ 2800	10.25 to 1	340	4-barrel	Premium

THE TRANSMISSIONS:

Regular Equipment	Option
3-speed Manual (Column Shift)	Automatic SuperTurbine (2-speed Column Shift) (3-speed available with "400" option and 340-4 eng.)

REAR AXLE RATIOS:

3-Speed Manual Trans. 3.36	SuperTurbine 2.93

EXTERIOR DIMENSIONS: (Approximations in inches.)

	Length	Width	Height	Wheelbase	Tread-front	Tread-rear
Sport Coupe	217.5	80.0	54.8	123.0	63.0	63.0
4-Door Hardtop	217.5	80.0	54.7	123.0	63.0	63.0
4-Door Sedan	217.5	80.0	55.6	123.0	63.0	63.0
Convertible	217.5	80.0	54.7	123.0	63.0	63.0

INTERIOR DIMENSIONS: (Approximations in inches.)

	Head Room		Leg Room		Shoulder Room	
	Front	Rear	Front	Rear	Front	Rear
Sport Coupe	38.4	37.2	42.3	34.9	62.2	61.0
4-Door Hardtop	38.1	37.3	42.2	38.5	62.3	61.4
4-Door Sedan	38.9	37.7	42.2	39.0	62.3	61.4
Convertible	39.0	37.9	42.3	34.9	62.2	53.1

SOME GOOD READING: Engine Lubricating System: Main bearings, connecting rods and camshaft bearings pressure lubricated. Cylinder walls splash and nozzle lubricated. Normal oil pressure 33 @ 2400. Full-flow oil filter. Crankcase

---

capacity (refill less filter) 4 quarts. **Fuel System:** Automatic choke. Mechanical fuel pump. Two-stage gasoline filter with fine filter in fuel tank. Oil impregnated polyurethane air cleaner. Exhaust type intake manifold heat control. **Capacity:** approximately 25 gallons. **Engine Cooling:** Pressure system. Choke-type circulation thermostat. Centrifugal water pump. Capacity: 12.2 quarts with heater. **Exhaust System:** Muffler constructed of corrosion resistant aluminized steel to promote longer life. **Electrical:** Twelve volt electrical system. Four-position starter-ignition switch. **Automatic Transmissions:** (optional) SuperTurbine is a torque converter type featuring a variable pitch stator within the converter; and a single planetary gear set or two planetary gear sets. Total oil capacity refill 19 pints. **Propeller Shaft:** Drive shaft is slightly angled to reduce tunnel height in rear seat. Angled sections are connected by a special constant-velocity universal joint that minimizes vibration during transfer of power to rear axle. Shaft is connected to transmission and rear axle by needle-bearing universal joints. **Rear Axle:** Hypoid gears, semi-floating. Transfer of driving forces through rubber-mounted arms connected to frame. **Frame:** Perimeter-type. **Suspension:** Independent ball-joint front suspension with link-type stabilizer bar. Four-link-type rear suspension. Coil springs front and rear. Direct acting hydraulic shock absorbers front and rear. **Brakes:** Hydraulic, self-energizing. Air-cooled finned brake drums front and rear. Total gross lining area 193.3 sq. in. Step-on parking brake operating through rear service brake shoes. Power brakes optional. **Tires:** 8.45 x 15. Optional tires available for other than normal driving conditions. Consult your Buick dealer. **Steering:** Manual recirculating ball steering standard. Overall ratio: 33.0 to 1. Easy Power Steering optional. Overall ratio: 20.5 to 1. Flexible coupling in power gear screens out road irregularities.

SPORTWAGON REGULAR EQUIPMENT—220-hp. 340-2 V-8; 3-speed Manual Transmission (Synchronized in all forward gears); Heater and Defroster; Re-usable Air Cleaner Element; Seat Belts—Front and Rear; Directional Signals; Cigar Lighter; Front Door-operated Courtesy Light; Ash Trays—Front and Rear; Ash Tray and Glove Compartment Light; Dual Side Arm Rests—Front and Rear; Dual-Key Locking System; Plunger-type Door Locks; Step-On Parking Brake; Magic-Mirror Finish; Deluxe Wheel Covers; Full-Flow Oil Filter; Dual Horns; 6,000-mile Lubed Front Suspension; Delcotron Generator; 14-inch Wheels; Self-adjusting Brakes; Cross-Flow Radiator; Upper Instrument Panel Pad; Outside Rear View Mirror; Dual Speed Windshield Wiper and Windshield Washer; Padded Sun Visors; Back-up Lamps. Deluxe Steering Wheel; Carpeting in Passenger Area; Custom Interior Trim; Custom Padded Seat Cushions.
NOTE: All Buick models feature the basic safety equipment listed on pages 12 and 13 as standard.

THE STANDARD ENGINE: 340-2

Horsepower	Torque	Compression Ratio	Displacement	Carburetion	Fuel
220 @ 4200	340 @ 2400	9.0 to 1	340	2-barrel	Regular

THE OPTIONAL ENGINE: 340-4

Horsepower	Torque	Compression Ratio	Displacement	Carburetion	Fuel
260 @ 4200	365 @ 2800	10.25 to 1	340	4-barrel	Premium

THE TRANSMISSIONS:

Regular Equipment	Option
3-speed Manual (Column Shift)	Automatic SuperTurbine (2-speed Column Shift) (3-speed available with "400" option and 340-4 engine)

REAR AXLE RATIOS:

3-Speed Manual Trans. 3.23	SuperTurbine 3.23

EXTERIOR DIMENSIONS: (Approximations in inches.)

Length	Width	Height	Wheelbase	Tread-front	Tread-rear
214.3	75.4	58.8	120.0	58.0	59.0

INTERIOR DIMENSIONS: (Approximations in inches.)

	Head Room		Leg Room		Shoulder Room	
	Front	Rear	Front	Rear	Front	Rear
2-Seat	37.9	40.5	41.3	38.7	58.2	58.0
3-Seat	37.9	39.1	41.3	37.0	58.2	58.0

SOME GOOD READING: Engine Lubricating System: Main bearings, connecting rods and camshaft bearings pressure lubricated. Cylinder walls splash and nozzle lubricated. Normal oil pressure 33 @ 2400. Full-flow oil filter. Crankcase capacity (refill less filter) 4 quarts. **Fuel System:** Automatic choke. Mechanical fuel pump. Two-stage gasoline filter with fine filter in fuel tank. Oil impregnated polyurethane air cleaner. Exhaust type intake manifold heat control. Approximately twenty gallon fuel capacity. **Engine Cooling:** Pressure system. Choke-type thermostat. Centrifugal water pump. Capacity: 12.2 quarts with heater. **Exhaust System:** Single muffler for both banks of cylinders. Constructed of corrosion resistant aluminized steel to promote longer life. **Electrical:** Twelve volt electrical system. Four-position starter-ignition switch. **Automatic Transmissions** (optional): SuperTurbine is of the torque converter type featuring a variable pitch stator within the converter, and a single planetary gear set or two planetary gear sets. Total oil capacity 19 pints or 22 pints. **Propeller Shaft:** Drive shaft is slightly angled to reduce tunnel height. Shaft is connected to transmission and rear axle by needle-bearing universal joints. **Rear Axle:** Hypoid gears, semi-floating. Rear wheel bearings permanently lubricated. **Suspension:** Independent ball-joint front suspension. Four-link rear suspension. Coil springs front and rear. Direct acting hydraulic shock absorbers front and rear. Driving forces from axle to frame are through rubber-bushed rear links. **Frame:** Perimeter-type. **Brakes:** Self-adjusting. Air-cooled finned aluminum front, alloy iron brake drums rear. Total gross lining area 175.6 sq. in. Parking brake operating through rear service brake shoes. Power brakes optional at extra cost. **Steering:** Manual recirculating ball steering standard. Overall ratio 28.6 to 1. Power steering optional. Overall ratio 20.9 to 1. **Tires:** 8.25 x 14. Optional tires are available for other than normal driving conditions. Consult your Buick...

A stableful of the finest thoroughbreds ever assembled: the Buick engines for 1967.

Two brand new engines are making their first runs on the track: the magnificent 430-4 and 400-4. Both have been bred and trained to deliver the finest performance you've ever seen. The all-new 430-4 is off and running with greater engine breathing capacity and improved fuel economy. Buick engineers have packed 360 horsepower into approximately the same size package as last year's 401 engine. Redesigned manifold and quadrajet carburetor have been tuned to larger cylinder head ports. New reusable air cleaners have lower air restriction and reusable filter elements. It's standard on all Rivieras, Electra 225s and Wildcats.

As a running mate, the new 400-4 puts an all-new series, the GS-400, in a performance class of its own. Quadrajet power and lower restriction air intake manifold and air cleaner work to produce an effortless 340 horsepower from this champion-sired new engine.

Two brand new blue bloods plus the great stable of V-8 and V-6 power provide the widest performance range yet. New crankshafts, special rocker arm and shaft assemblies, rotating valve lifters, new radiators, new exhaust systems, new fuel indicators, new locations for distributors and coils, new oil filter assemblies, new harmonic balancers, new rocker arm covers . . . the list of improvements goes on and on. Winners even finer than the 1966 Buick engines that paced the field in the Pure Oil Performance Trials and Mobil Economy Run . . . that remain the choice of leading marine engine builders and fabricators. Six to one your favorite's right here.

400-4. V-8.
Horsepower: 340 @ 5000.
Torque: 440 @ 3200.
Compression ratio: 10.25 to 1.
Displacement: 400 cu. in.
Carburetion: 4-barrel.
Fuel: Premium.
Standard on GS-400.

A tour of the Buick stables: 1,550 of the world's best-bred horses.

340-4. V-8.
Horsepower: 260 @ 4200.
Torque: 365 @ 2800.
Compression ratio: 10.25 to 1.
Displacement: 340 cu. in.
Carburetion: 4-barrel.
Fuel: Premium.
Standard on Custom Sportwagon with "400" package.
Standard on LeSabre with "400" package.
Available on all Special, Special Deluxe, Skylark, Sportwagon and LeSabre models.

340-2. V-8.
Horsepower: 220 @ 4200.
Torque: 340 @ 2400.
Compression ratio: 9.0 to 1.
Displacement: 340 cu. in.
Carburetion: 2-barrel.
Fuel: Regular.
Standard on Sportwagon, LeSabre, and Skylark 4-door hardtop.

300-2. V-8.
Horsepower: 210 @ 4400.
Torque: 310 @ 2400.
Compression ratio: 9.0 to 1.
Displacement: 300 cu. in.
Carburetion: 2-barrel.
Fuel: Regular.
Standard on Special Deluxe Wagon, Skylark Sport Coupe and Skylark convertible.
Available on all Special, Special Deluxe Sport Coupe and 4-door sedan and Skylark 2-door Thin Pillar Coupe models.

225-2. V-6.
Horsepower: 160 @ 4200.
Torque: 235 @ 2400.
Compression ratio: 9.0 to 1.
Displacement: 225 cu. in.
Carburetion: 2-barrel.
Fuel: Regular.
Standard on all Special, Special Deluxe Sport Coupe and 4-door sedan and Skylark 2-door Thin Pillar Coupe models.

(Shown on facing page)
430-4. V-8.
Horsepower: 360 @ 5000.
Torque: 475 @ 3200.
Compression ratio: 10.25 to 1.
Displacement: 430 cu. in.
Carburetion: 4-barrel.
Fuel: Premium.
Standard on Riviera, Electra 225, Wildcat.

THE WILDCAT INTERIORS

Custom Wildcat interior features Madrid grain vinyl notchback — beautifully contoured for maximum driving comfort. Available in the sport coupe and 4-door hardtop sedan in blue, dove, aqua or black and the convertible in blue, dove, red or black. Other luxury touches are upper and lower door panel moldings of extruded aluminum, a center panel molding of horizontally brushed aluminum and carpeting that covers the lower portion of the door on 2-door models. You can also order Madrid grain vinyl bucket seats in black that recline on the passenger side and a shifting console as optional equipment.

"Know this guy?
It's Bill Bixby, star of MGM's
'Doctor, You've Got To Be Kidding.'
Bill is best known for his
TV role in 'My Favorite Martian'
—a logical place to develop
a taste for out-of-this-world
transportation."

(SOME OF THE EQUIPMENT SHOWN ON THE CAR ILLUSTRATED IS OPTIONAL AT EXTRA COST.)
MR. BIXBY CAN ALSO BE SEEN IN COLUMBIA PICTURE'S "RIDE BEYOND VENGEANCE"

Wildcat Custom Sport Coupe.

Doesn't this convince you that you need
a new car this year?

We can think of just one thing greater than
the Wildcat you're driving today:
the Wildcat you'll be driving tomorrow.

Wildcat Custom 4-dr. Hardtop.

Wildcat Custom Convertible.
Now you know why
summer is the most wonderful time of the year.

Buick Wildcat Regular Equipment:

360-hp. 430-4 V8 engine; 3-speed manual transmission (synchronized in all forward gears); heater and defroster; self-adjusting brakes; finned aluminum front brake drums with cast iron liners; dual master cylinder brake system with warning light and corrosion resistant brake lines; seat belts with pushbutton buckles for *all* passenger positions; shoulder belts with push-button buckles and special storage convenience provision for driver and right front passenger (except convertibles); step-on parking brake; four-way hazard warning flasher; directional signals; lane change feature in direction signal control; front door-operated interior light; glove compartment light; smoking set; rear seat ash trays; Magic-Mirror finish; safety arm rests —front and rear; 15-inch wheels; dual horns; crank-operated vent windows; soft, low-profile window control knobs and coat hooks; 6,000-mile lubed front suspension; Delcotron generator; carpeting; dual-key locking system; Full-Flow oil filter; passenger guard door locks with deflecting lock buttons—all doors; folding seat back latches; custom interior trims (Wildcat Custom models); deluxe steering wheel; energy absorbing steering column; paddle-type arm rest (Wildcat Custom models); custom headlining (Wildcat Custom models—except Convertible); cross-flow radiator; padded instrument panel, sun visors, windshield corner posts; reduced glare instrument panel top, inside windshield mouldings, horn control, steering wheel hub, and windshield wiper arms and blades; thick laminate windshield; padded front and intermediate seat back tops and lower structure; recessed dual-speed windshield wipers; windshield washers; backup lights, new side marker lights and parking lamps that illuminate with headlamps; inside day-night mirror with deflecting base—outside rear view mirror; yielding smooth contoured door and window regulator handles.

NOTE: All Buick models feature the safety equipment listed on pages 36 and 37 as standard.

THE STANDARD ENGINE: 430-4 V8.

Horsepower	Torque	Compression Ratio	Displacement	Carburetion	Fuel
360 @ 5000	475 @ 3200	10.25 to 1	430	4-barrel	Premium

THE TRANSMISSIONS:

Regular Equipment 3-Speed Manual (Column Mounted)	*Option* Automatic Super Turbine (Column or Console Mounted)

REAR AXLE RATIOS:

3-Speed Manual Transmission	*Automatic Super Turbine*
3.07	3.07

Consult your Buick dealer for information on optional ratios.

EXTERIOR DIMENSIONS: (Approximations in inches.)

	Length	Width	Height	Wheelbase	Tread-front	Tread-rear
Sport Coupe	220.46	80.0	55.2	126.0	63.44	63.0
4-Door Hardtop	220.46	80.0	55.2	126.0	63.44	63.0
4-Door Sedan	220.46	80.0	55.3	126.0	63.44	63.0
Convertible	220.46	80.0	55.2	126.0	63.44	63.0

INTERIOR DIMENSIONS: (Approximations in inches.)

	Head Room		Leg Room		Shoulder Room	
	Front	Rear	Front	Rear	Front	Rear
Sport Coupe	38.7	37.3	42.2	34.9	62.2	61.0
4-Door Hardtop	38.7	37.8	42.2	38.5	62.3	61.4
4-Door Sedan	39.6	38.3	42.2	39.0	62.3	61.4
Convertible	38.8	37.9	42.1	34.9	62.2	53.1

MORE IMPORTANT INFORMATION ABOUT THE WILDCAT: **Engine Lubricating System:** Main bearings, connecting rods and camshaft bearings pressure lubricated. Cylinder walls splash and nozzle lubricated. Normal oil pressure 40 @ 2400. Full-Flow oil filter. Crankcase capacity (refill less filter) 4 quarts. **Fuel System:** Automatic choke. Mechanical fuel pump. Pleated paper gasoline filter with fine filter in fuel tank. Oiled paper element air cleaner. Exhaust-type intake manifold heat control. Fuel Tank Capacity: approximately 25 gallons. **Engine Cooling:** Pressure system. Choke-type circulation thermostat. Centrifugal water pump. Capacity: 16.7 quarts with heater. **Exhaust System:** Muffler constructed of corrosion resistant aluminized steel to promote longer life. Dual exhaust available as optional equipment with automatic transmission. **Electrical:** Twelve-volt electrical system. Four-position starter-ignition switch. **Automatic Transmission:** Super Turbine is of a torque converter type. Total oil capacity 23 pints. **Propeller Shaft:** Drive shaft is slightly angled to reduce tunnel height in rear seat. Angled sections are connected by a special constant-velocity universal joint that minimizes vibration during transfer of power to rear axle. Shaft is connected to transmission and rear axle by needle-bearing universal joints. **Rear Axle:** Hypoid gears, semi-floating. Transfer of driving forces through rubber-mounted arms connected to frame. **Frame:** Perimeter type. **Suspension:** Independent ball-joint front suspension with link-type stabilizer bar. Four-link-type rear suspension. Coil springs front and rear. Direct acting hydraulic shock absorbers front and rear. **Brakes:** Hydraulic, self-energizing. Air-cooled finned aluminum front brake drums with cast iron liners; finned drums rear. Total gross lining area 193.3 sq. in. Step-on parking brake operating through rear service brake shoes. Power brakes optional. **Tires:** 8.45 x 15. Optional tires available for other than normal driving conditions. Consult your Buick dealer. **Steering:** Manual recirculating ball, standard. Easy power steering, optional. Overall ratio: 18.9 to 1. Flexible coupling in power gear screens out road irregularities.

Wildcat Interiors.
Is that a smile we see on your face?

The excitement you felt the minute you set eyes on your new Wildcat Sport Coupe had only just begun. Open the door. Climb inside. And, if anything, you'll be more excited than ever.

You'll sit there for a moment. Enjoying the luxury of deep, foam-padded seats. Grasping the Deluxe Steering Wheel. If you've equipped your Wildcat with the optional Tilt Steering Wheel, you'll probably adjust it to all six positions.

You'll look out over Wildcat's clean, graceful hood. Then you'll begin looking around you. Inspecting. Enjoying.

You'll notice the front and rear seat belts and front shoulder belts that are standard equipment this year. You'll check the thick carpeting beneath your feet. You'll study the unique instrument panel. Feel the thick foam padding. Try the treadle switches that are new in the '68 Wildcat. Try all the controls.

Maybe you'll have equipped your Wildcat with 6-way power bench seats. You'll try all positions. Maybe you'll have power windows. Air conditioning. A stereo tape player. You'll test all of them.

Instead of bench seats in your Hardtop Coupe or Convertible, you may have All-Vinyl Bucket seats. With an automatic transmission. And a full-length floor console. You'll try the easy movement of the control lever.

Whatever equipment you've ordered in your '68 Wildcat, it will be precisely what you've always wanted in a car.

That's the kind of car a Wildcat is. The kind of car you've always wanted.

The first time you sit behind the wheel of your own Wildcat, you'll know it.

Custom All-Vinyl Bucket Seats.

Cloth-and-Vinyl Bench Seat.

Now you have to choose what you're going to sit on. What style seats. What colors.

And you have quite a list to choose from.

☐ Sport Coupe. You can equip your Wildcat Sport Coupe with Cloth-and-Vinyl Bench seats, blue or champagne. With All-Vinyl Bench seats in blue, black, buckskin or platinum. Or with black All-Vinyl Bucket seats.

☐ Hardtop Sedan. Cloth-and-Vinyl Bench seats are standard. Available in platinum, blue, maroon or champagne. If you wish, choose All-Vinyl Bench seats, blue, black or buckskin.

☐ Sedan. Select from the same choices as offered on the Hardtop Sedan.

☐ Custom Sport Coupe. All-Vinyl Notch-Back seats are standard. In blue, white, platinum or black. Or you can order black All-Vinyl Bucket seats.

☐ Custom Hardtop Sedan. Cloth-and-Vinyl Notch-Back seats are standard. In blue or black. All-Vinyl Notch-Back seats are available in blue, white, platinum or black.

☐ Custom Convertible. All-Vinyl Notch-Back seats are standard equipment on the Wildcat Custom Convertible. Four colors are available: blue, white, red or black. You can choose black All-Vinyl Bucket seats, if you like.

Custom Cloth-and-Vinyl Notch-Back Seat.

Buick 1969

The penultimate Wildcat did not receive extensive changes from its predecessor. The annual facelift still kept some of the trim items, retaining the Wildcat's uniqueness.

The same body types were repeated for 1969, as well as the base and Custom versions. Prices rose about $75. The new price spread was from $3,491 for the four-door sedan to $3,948 for the convertible.

The convertible was the rarest 1969 Wildcat model—2,374 having been built. The five other models were almost equal in popularity. Production ranged from 13,805 four-door sedans to 12,136 Custom two-door Sport Coupes. Production was down for the model year, but not by much. There were 67,453 Wildcats made during the model year.

The Riviera/Electra engine continued to power the Wildcat in a more than adequate manner. It was virtually unchanged, so still developed 360 advertised hp. The transmission choices were also very similar to the preceding year. A 3-speed column mounted manual transmission was standard. A 3-speed automatic, with column or console mounted lever, was on the option list. Top speed remained at 120 mph as reported by the "World Car Catalog."

Another big 74 page full-line catalogue was issued by Buick. A smaller and more condensed edition was also published, as well as a much different thin black catalogue featuring color photography more than technical data. The Wildcat got its share in each of these brochures.

Returning from the Electra chassis to that of the restyled LeSabre, the 1970 Wildcat was back in its familiar niche. This was to be its last year, and the Wildcat went all the way with a 455 cubic inch engine. It was the biggest ever installed in a Wildcat or any other production Buick. This was the same engine which made a simultaneous debut in the Riviera and Electra, as well. It developed 370 hp and 510 foot/pounds of torque. However, top speed was not up to what it had been. It was 115 mph, so the "World Cars Catalog" reported.

The model line-up for its last year was cut in half, by dropping the base series. Only the Wildcat Custom was offered, in the two hardtops and convertible body types. There were just 1,244 Wildcat convertibles built in the final model year. The most popular of the final Wildcats were the 12,924 four-door hardtops built. Production was way down in its concluding year, just 23,615 Wildcats were made.

Slowing demand for the final Wildcat was a price hike of nearly $300. For the first time, base prices were above $4,000—all above $4,100 in fact. The two-door Sport Coupe was $4,107, the four-door hardtop $4,155, and the convertible $4,237.

The usual, large, full-line Buick catalogue was accompanied by two versions of a much smaller catalogue. The Wildcat Custom was included in each of these brochures.

The literature excerpted in this chapter includes the 1969 and 1970 full-line showroom catalogues (see pages 106-109 and 112-121, respectively). The cover of the 1969 saver brochure is reproduced on page 104, while an excerpt from the 1969 "Decisions, decisions, decisions" mailer catalogue is reproduced on pages 110-111.

1969 Buick Wildcat

Our Buick buffs will tell you that Wildcat really earns its name and reputation. Oh, Wildcat has more than its share of Buick luxury, all right. But this Buick is sporting more than just luxury.

Wildcat is the youngest, the sportiest of all the big Buicks. A lot of people think Wildcat is the poshest performance machine on the road. You'll probably think so yourself after your first ride in this great new Buick.

The Wildcat look? A bit more spirited, more rakish than anything else in its class, wouldn't you say?

Wildcat performance? Just take a Wildcat out on the road. Discover all the effortless response you can ask for from Wildcat's big 430-4 V8.

How about Wildcat's handling and braking? You'll find nothing short of the best in handling and braking equipment to complement Wildcat's total performance. Big front and rear coil springs, direct acting shock absorbers, Wildcat's new Directional Stability System (DSS) and power disc brakes are just a few of the features that make Wildcat one of the straightest trackers and safest stoppers in the industry.

Still with us? Then you're obviously the type who can't resist a go at a car like the 1969 Wildcat. See for yourself how well soft luxury mates with superb performance. In a 1969 Buick Wildcat.

Wildcat Interiors:

Sunday morning! What a day for that drive you've been promising the family. And now you're going to do it in style. 1969 Wildcat style.

A day like this makes you glad you chose a Wildcat, doesn't it? Especially now that you're relaxing on rugged Vinyl seats, almost ready to start the wheels turning.

You press forward on the six-way Power Seat Control you ordered for your Wildcat and bring yourself closer to the action. You adjust the tilt steering wheel just a notch. You flick on your Wildcat's AM/FM stereo radio. Something on the upbeat side comes on crystal strong. What a Sunday this is going to be!

Remember when you were choosing between the Wildcat Custom Sport Coupe, the Hardtop Sedan and the Custom Convertible? Between the bucket seats and full-length console, the Automatic Climate Control and all the other Wildcat options and accessories? Well it looks like you made all the right moves when you chose your brand of Wildcat, doesn't it?

Of course, any of the 1969 Wildcats would have made this a great Sunday to go Wildcatting, wouldn't they?

Everybody set? Come on, Wildcat. Make tracks!

Buick Wildcat Custom Sport Coupe

Custom Vinyl
Notch-Back Seat

Here's the colorful inside story on the 1969 Wildcats.

Sport Coupe. Kimberly Cloth-and-Vinyl Bench Seats in green, buckskin or blue are standard. Or choose Vinyl Bench Seats in blue, black, buckskin or pearl white.

Hardtop Sedan and Sedan. Select standard Kimberly Cloth-and-Vinyl Bench Seat in blue, green, or buckskin. Or specify Vinyl Bench Seat in blue, black, buckskin or pearl white.

Custom Sport Coupe. Vinyl Notch-Back Seats available in pearl white, buckskin, blue or black. Or select black Vinyl Bucket Seats.

Custom Hardtop Sedan. Kilmer Cloth-and-Vinyl Notch-Back Seats in sandalwood or black. Or Vinyl Notch-Back Seats in blue, buckskin, pearl white or black are standard.

Custom Convertible. Vinyl Notch-Back Seats in pearl white or black are standard.

Some of the equipment illustrated or described is optional at extra cost.

Cloth-and-Vinyl Bench Seat

Custom Vinyl Bucket Seats

Wildcat Regular Equipment:

Power Train: 360 hp 430-4 engine; 3-speed manual transmission (synchronized in all forward gears); Delcotron generator; Full-Flow oil filter; cross-flow radiator.

Handling and Braking Features: self-adjusting brakes; finned aluminum front brake drums with cast iron liners; 15-inch wheels; 6,000-mile lubed front suspension; independent ball-joint front suspension with link-type stabilizer bar; Tru-Trac directional stability system.

Safety Equipment: energy-absorbing steering column; two front-seat head restraints; passenger-guard door locks—with forward-mounted lock button; latches on folding seatbacks; dual-action safety hood latch; outside rearview mirror; wide inside day-night mirror with deflecting base; anti-theft ignition, steering and transmission lock; starter switch on all transmissions—manual and automatic; "Cargo-guard" luggage compartment; contoured windshield header (except convertibles); seatbelts with pushbutton buckles for all passenger positions; driver and right front passenger shoulder belts with pushbutton buckles and special storage provision (except convertibles); four-way hazard warning flasher; dual master cylinder brake system with warning light and corrosion-resistant brake lines; windshield washer and dual-speed wipers; back-up lights; side marker lights and parking lights that illuminate with headlights; energy-absorbing instrument panel; padded sun visors; reduced-glare instrument panel top; inside windshield moldings; horn buttons, steering wheel hub, and windshield wiper arms and blades; lane-change feature in direction signal control; safety armrests; thick-laminate windshield; soft, low-profile window control knobs; coat hooks and dome lights; padded front and intermediate seatback tops; smooth-contoured door and window regulator handles; anti-theft ignition key warning buzzer.

Comfort and Convenience Equipment: upper level ventilation; heater and defroster; front door-operated interior light; glove compartment light; smoking set; rear seat ash trays; Magic-Mirror finish; arm rests—front and rear; carpeting; custom interior trims (Wildcat Custom models); deluxe steering wheel; custom headlining (Wildcat Custom models—except convertibles).

The Wildcat engine at rest. A flick of the key, a touch of the pedal puts you in command of 360 horses' worth of thoroughbred V8!

Wildcat Custom Four-Door Hardtop and Wildcat Custom Convertible

THE STANDARD ENGINE: 430-4 V8

Horsepower	Torque	Compression Ratio	Displacement	Carburetion	Fuel
360 @ 5000	475 @ 3200	10.25	430	4-barrel	Premium

THE TRANSMISSIONS:

Regular Equipment 3-Speed Manual   Optional 3-Speed Turbo-Hydramatic 400
(Column Mounted)   (Column or Console Mounted)

REAR AXLE RATIOS:

3-Speed Manual Transmission   Turbo-Hydramatic
3.07   3.07

Consult your Buick dealer for information on optional ratios.

EXTERIOR DIMENSIONS: (Approximations in inches.)

	Length	Width	Height	Wheelbase	Tread-front	Tread-rear
Sport Coupe	218.2	80.0	54.6	123.2	63.5	63.0
4-Door Hardtop	218.2	80.0	54.3	123.2	63.5	63.0
4-Door Sedan	218.2	80.0	55.0	123.2	63.5	63.0
Convertible	218.2	80.0	54.9	123.2	63.5	63.0

APPROX. CURB WEIGHT: (Wildcat Four-Door) 4,313 lbs.

INTERIOR DIMENSIONS: (Approximations in inches.)

	Head Room		Leg Room		Shoulder Room	
	Front	Rear	Front	Rear	Front	Rear
Sport Coupe	38.4	37.7	42.2	33.9	61.7	60.3
4-Door Hardtop	38.1	37.4	42.2	37.5	61.6	60.8
4-Door Sedan	38.9	37.7	42.2	37.9	61.6	60.7
Convertible	38.9	37.9	42.2	33.9	62.2	52.3

MORE IMPORTANT INFORMATION ABOUT THE WILDCAT: **Engine Lubricating System:** Main bearings, connecting rods and camshaft bearings pressure lubricated. Cylinder walls splash and nozzle lubricated. Normal oil pressure 40 @ 2400. Full-Flow oil filter. Crankcase capacity (refill less filter) 3.3 quarts. **Fuel System:** Automatic choke. Mechanical fuel pump. Pleated paper gasoline filter with fine filter in fuel tank. Wider diameter oiled paper element air cleaner. Exhaust-type intake manifold heat control. Fuel Tank Capacity: approximately 20.5 gallons. **Engine Cooling:** Pressure system. Choke-type circulation thermostat. Centrifugal water pump. Capacity: 14 quarts. **Exhaust System:** Single exhaust with crossover standard. Duals available. **Electrical:** Twelve-volt electrical system. Four-position starter-ignition switch. **Automatic Transmission:** Turbo-Hydramatic is of a torque converter type. Total oil capacity 20 pints. **Propeller Shaft:** Shaft is connected to transmission and rear axle by needle-bearing universal joints. **Rear Axle:** Hypoid gears, semi-floating. Transfer of driving forces through rubber-mounted arms connected to frame. **Frame:** Perimeter type. **Suspension:** Independent ball-joint Tru-Trac front suspension with link-type stabilizer bar. Coil springs front and rear. Direct acting hydraulic shock absorbers front and rear. **Brakes:** Hydraulic. Air-cooled finned aluminum front brake drums with cast iron liners; finned-drums rear. Total gross lining area 193.3 sq. in. Step-on parking brake operating through rear service brake shoes. Power brakes optional. **Tires:** 8.55 x 15. Optional tires available for other than normal driving conditions. Consult your Buick dealer. **Steering:** Manual recirculating ball, overall ratio: 34.3 standard. Power steering. (Optional with overall variable ratio: 19.6-14.0.) Flexible coupling in power gear screens out road irregularities.

Some of the equipment illustrated or described is optional at extra cost.

Wildcat... A new thoroughbred!

You're off and running with Wildcat! The youngest, sportiest of all big Buicks. One that puts posh and performance together in a way to make you purr with delight. Under the hood, a 430 cubic inch powerplant is ready to spirit you to lands of adventure. For handling and performance, it's hard to match Wildcat. Features include finned aluminum front brakes . . . durable direct-acting shock absorbers with Teflon seals . . . and new directional stability. Wildcat is for the man . . . or woman . . . on the move. Excitement in every line . . . ecstasy in every look. How about you? Are you ready to go Wildcatting?

Wildcat Custom 4-dr. Hardtop

There are six Wildcat delightful decisions waiting for you in all. They include the Wildcat Sport Coupe, $3579; Wildcat 4-dr. Sedan, $3474; Wildcat 4-dr. Hardtop, $3634; Wildcat Custom Sport Coupe, $3800; Wildcat Custom 4-dr. Hardtop, $3849; and Wildcat Custom Convertible, $3931.*

Above is a Wildcat Custom 4-dr. Hardtop priced at $3849.* Add for options shown: Custom Vinyl Top, $121.04; Sonomatic Radio with Electric Antenna, $117.88; Whitewall Tires, $42.21; Chrome-plated Wheels, $94.73; Cornering Lights, $33.68; Protective Side Mouldings, $33.68; Door Edge Guards, $8.95; Head Restraints, $16.84; and Remote Control Mirror, $10.53.

*Manufacturer's Suggested Retail Prices include Federal excise tax and suggested dealer delivery and handling charge. Option prices include Federal excise tax. Destination charge, state and local taxes are extra.

The country gentleman steadying his steed is sporting a Neiman-Marcus exclusive—a sueded pigskin jacket from West Germany ($165.00) worn over a Scottish lambswool turtleneck ($25.00) and accented by an Austrian velours sports hat ($29.50). His partner is attired in a herringbone wool tweed country suit from France ($245.00) selected from the Neiman-Marcus Trophy Room collection.

Wildcat Custom Sport Coupe

Some of the equipment shown is available at extra cost.

Wildcat Custom 4-door Hardtop.

Wildcat Custom Convertible.

Some of the equipment shown is available at extra cost.

Keswick Cloth-and-Vinyl Notch-Back Seat is available at no extra
cost on the Wildcat Custom Hardtop Sedan in Sandalwood or Black.

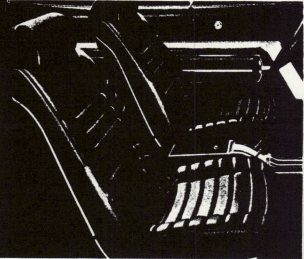

Black All-Vinyl Bucket Seats are available at no extra cost on the Wildcat
Custom Sport Coupe.

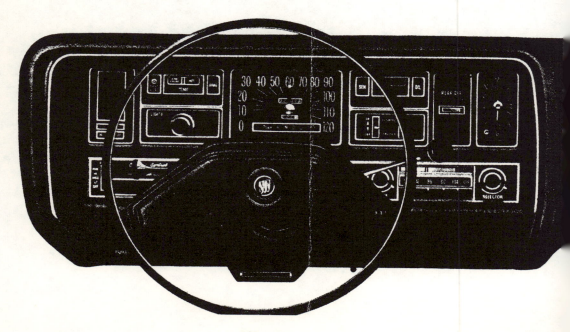

1970 Wildcat Custom Regular Equipment

Power Train: 370 hp 455-4 V8 engine; three-speed manual transmission fully-synchronized in all forward gears; Delcotron generator; Full-Flow oil filter; new semi-closed cooling system.

Handling and Braking Features: self-adjusting brakes with finned aluminum front brake drums with cast iron liners; gross lining area 193.3 sq. in.; 6,000 mile lubed front suspension; Buick's Accu-Drive suspension system; H78 x 15 Fiberglas belted tires; direct-acting hydraulic shock absorbers.

Comfort and Convenience Equipment: Comfort-Flo ventilating system; heater and defroster; front door-operated interior light; glove compartment light; smoking set; rear seat ash trays; Magic-Mirror finish; arm rests—front and rear carpeting; custom interior trims; deluxe steering wheel.

THE STANDARD ENGINE: 455-4 V8.

Horsepower	Torque	Compression Ratio	Displacement	Carburetion	Fuel
370 @ 4600	510 @ 2800	10.0	455	4-barrel	Premium

THE TRANSMISSIONS:

Regular Equipment: 3-Speed Manual (Column Shift)

Available: 3-Speed Turbo-Hydramatic 400 Automatic Transmission (Column or Console Mounted Shift)

REAR AXLE RATIOS:

3-Speed Manual Transmission: 2.78   Automatic: 2.78

Consult your Buick dealer for information on available ratios.

EXTERIOR DIMENSIONS: (Approximations in inches.)

	Length	Width	Height	Wheelbase
Sport Coupe	220.2	80.0	54.7	124.0
4-Door Hardtop	220.2	80.0	54.4	124.0
Convertible	220.2	80.0	54.6	124.0

INTERIOR DIMENSIONS: (Approximations in inches.)

	Head Room		Leg Room		Shoulder Room	
	Front	Rear	Front	Rear	Front	Rear
Sport Coupe	37.8	37.2	42.2	33.9	62.2	60.8
4-Door Hardtop	37.6	36.9	42.2	37.5	62.2	61.3
Convertible	38.5	37.9	42.2	33.9	62.2	52.3

Some of the equipment shown or described is available at extra cost.

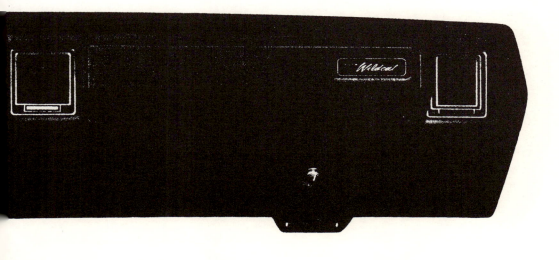

1970 Wildcat Custom Regular Equipment

Power Train: 370 hp 455-4 V8 engine; three-speed manual transmission fully-synchronized in all forward gears; Delcotron generator; Full-Flow oil filter; new semi-closed cooling system.

Handling and Braking Features: self-adjusting brakes with finned aluminum front brake drums with cast iron liners; gross lining area 193.3 sq. in.; 6,000 mile lubed front suspension; Buick's Accu-Drive suspension system; H78 x 15 Fiberglas belted tires; direct-acting hydraulic shock absorbers.

Comfort and Convenience Equipment: Comfort-Flo ventilating system; heater and defroster; front door-operated interior light; glove compartment light; smoking set; rear seat ash trays; Magic-Mirror finish; arm rests—front and rear carpeting; custom interior trims; deluxe steering wheel.

THE STANDARD ENGINE: 455-4 V8.

Horsepower	Torque	Compression Ratio	Displacement	Carburetion	Fuel
370 @ 4600	510 @ 2800	10.0	455	4-barrel	Premium

THE TRANSMISSIONS:

Regular Equipment: 3-Speed Manual (Column Shift)

Available: 3-Speed Turbo-Hydramatic 400 Automatic Transmission (Column or Console Mounted Shift)

REAR AXLE RATIOS:

3-Speed Manual Transmission: 2.78   Automatic: 2.78

Consult your Buick dealer for information on available ratios.

EXTERIOR DIMENSIONS: (Approximations in inches.)

	Length	Width	Height	Wheelbase
Sport Coupe	220.2	80.0	54.7	124.0
4-Door Hardtop	220.2	80.0	54.4	124.0
Convertible	220.2	80.0	54.6	124.0

INTERIOR DIMENSIONS: (Approximations in inches.)

	Head Room		Leg Room		Shoulder Room	
	Front	Rear	Front	Rear	Front	Rear
Sport Coupe	37.8	37.2	42.2	33.9	62.2	60.8
4-Door Hardtop	37.6	36.9	42.2	37.5	62.2	61.3
Convertible	38.5	37.9	42.2	33.9	62.2	52.3

1971-1973

The new name for the middle series of Buick's standard size cars was Centurion. It perpetuated the same tradition established by the Century and continued by the Invicta and Wildcat. It used Buick's biggest engine in a smaller body. In this case, it was literally Buick's biggest engine—the largest ever used in production.

Displacing 455 cubic inches, it developed 315 net hp. Although this was a version of the same motor the last Wildcat used, Federal government anti-pollution specifications were inhibiting power, so the 1971 rating of this engine was down 15% from the previous year. Probably for this reason, a so-called High Performance optional engine was offered. Of the same displacement, but with dual exhausts, the alternate engine was rated at 330 hp.

That was 100 more horses than the standard LeSabre had. So, the Centurion, using the same body, had a definite power advantage, even though it was 200 to 230 lbs heavier than the LeSabre.

In the minds of some people, the name Centurion was associated with the World War II tank and the connection was not totally absurd. The Buick Centurion was a huge and heavy vehicle. It weighed in at 4,200 lbs and stretched to over 220 inches in overall length, but it was not a cumbersome vehicle. "Road Test" magazine reported a 0 to 60 time of 10.3 seconds (using low and drive), a quarter mile time of 17.1 seconds at 80 mph and an estimated top speed of 115 mph. That was for a Centurion with the standard 315 hp motor.

The 1971 Centurion had its own distinctive grille, but did not bother with the fake port-holes on the side of the hood that the LeSabre, Estate Wagon and Electra had. The usual three body types were offered in the Centurion series. The two-door hardtop, called the Formal Coupe, and convertible each had a price tag of $4,678, while the four-door hardtop had a $4,564 list price. That was an increase of more than $400-$500 over similar 1970 Wildcat models.

The four-door hardtop, perhaps because of its lower relative price, was favored by the buyers, as 15,345 were produced. Only 2,161 Centurion convertibles were produced. A total of 29,398 Centurions were produced in its first model year. That was up nearly 25% over the Wildcat in its final model year.

The all-model 45 page horizontal catalogue for 1971 Buick had six pages describing, in text and illustrations, the Centurion and its options. No separate Centurion pieces were published.

In its 1972 season, the Centurion was 24% more popular than in its freshman year. Model year production reached 36,439, and 19,852 were four-door hardtops. The number of convertibles built was only 2,396.

The same standard and optional engines were available for 1972. However, a comparison of horsepower with the previous year is difficult to determine. Because of all the power-robbing, anti-pollution gear required, the car makers had to publish net hp, instead of the more meaningless gross hp figures. The 1972 Centurion engines were rated at 225 net hp for the standard engine, and 260 net hp for the optional version.

Only the Turbo Hydra-Matic 400 automatic transmission was obtainable in the 1972 Centurion. The 3-speed, column-mounted manual transmission, standard the year before, was no longer offered. The "World Cars" Catalog" stated the top speed, with the standard engine, was 105 mph. Poorer performance was the indirect result of government regulations concerning emissions.

As performance slipped slightly, prices also eased. The four-door hardtop sold for $4,508; the two-door Formula Coupe, $4,579; and the convertible, $4,616. That was $56 to $99 less than for 1971.

Eight pages of large color photographs and a succinct text told the Centurion story in the 50 page all-model 1972 Buick catalogue. There was no exclusive Centurion literature issued.

The third year of the Centurion, 1973, was its last. The trend for high-performance cars, already shrinking, had largely shifted to the mid-size class. Nevertheless, the momentum Buick had built up for nearly two decades with this type of car helped the Centurion to maintain, even increase, its popularity. There were 44,976 Centurions produced in the 1973 model year.

Virtually half of them—22,354—were four-door hardtops. Convertibles were the rarest, but production was up considerably to 5,739. Prices were reduced, for a second year, to a range from $4,336 to $4,534—down $82 to $243 from 1972.

There was a very noticeable retrenchment in power for 1973. The standard engine was only a 350 cubic inch V-8 that developed an anemic 175 net hp. However, the 455 cubic inch engines of before were still optionally available. They were rated at 225 and 250 net hp. Even the Centurion with standard power could reach a top speed of 106 mph. That is a respectable speed, but probably the slowest of all the Buicks this book describes.

When the last 1973 Centurion came off the assembly line, an exciting era had come to an end. That terminated Buick's production of high powered standard sized cars. From the 1954 Century to the 1973 Centurion, Buick had built more than one and a quarter million standard size hot cars. They were not silly kids' stuff.

As expected, the Centurion was included in the mid-size/full-size Buick catalogue. Also, as was Buick's habit, there was no Centurion-only literature printed.

Literature excepted in this chapter includes the full-line showroom catalogues for 1971, 1972 and 1973 (see pages 124-131, 132-137 and 138-143, respectively.)

Centurion

Centurion Formal Coupe.

Centurion Convertible.

Centurion 4-Door Hardtop Sedan.

Inside Centurion
Look. Feel. Touch. Everything is new. The 1971 Centurion Formal Coupe is unique in every exciting innovation and appointment. Comfortable interior dimensions await your pleasure.
Front head room: 38.1 inches;
Rear head room: 37.1 inches;
Front leg room: 42.6 inches;
Rear leg room: 35.5 inches;
Front shoulder room: 64.3 inches;
Rear shoulder room: 62.2 inches.

Outside Centurion
Distinctive vinyl top and formal roofline. New textured wide angle grill. Beauty in a word is Centurion. The following exterior dimensions are proof of its totally new design and styling. Length: 220.7 inches; Width: 79.7 inches; Height: 53.6 inches; Wheelbase 124.0 inches. (Note: Centurion exterior and interior specifications are approximations in inches.)

Centurion Performance
Sure-footed dependability, reliability. Something to believe in. Yours to command.
Standard engine: 455-4 V8; Compression ratio: 8.5:1; Displacement: 455 C.I.D.; Carburetion: 4-barrel.
Available engine: 455-4 (High Performance); dual exhausts.
Transmission: Standard: 3-speed manual (column shift mounted). Available: 3-speed Turbo Hydra-matic 400 Automatic Transmission.

Rear Axle Ratio: 3-speed manual: 3.42; 3-speed Automatic Transmission: 2.93. Consult your Buick dealer for information on available ratios.

Centurion Comfort
Experience convenience. Comfort. Centurion has an abundance of both: Full-Flo ventilation system; heater and defroster; front door-operated interior light; glove compartment light; smoking set; rear seat ash

---

Inside Centurion
Wide open and wonderful. Sit in; stretch out. Spacious comfort is yours in the all new 1971 Centurion Convertible as the following interior dimensions illustrate.
Front head room: 38.9 inches;
Rear head room: 38.1 inches;
Front leg room: 42.6 inches;
Rear leg room: 35.5 inches;
Front shoulder room: 62.2 inches;
Rear shoulder room: 61.7 inches.

Outside Centurion
Scene stealing design. Sleek and slim. Toss your cares to the wind. The 1971 Centurion Convertible is an experience you'll want to own. The following exterior dimensions should help you make your decision an easy one. Length: 220.7 inches; Width: 79.7 inches; Height: 53.9 inches; Wheelbase: 124.0 inches. (Note: Centurion interior and exterior dimensions are approximations in inches.)

Centurion Performance
Swift. Sure and secure. Buick dependability. Buick reliability. Something to believe in. Yours to command.
Standard engine: 455-4 V8; Compression ratio: 8.5:1; Displacement: 455 C.I.D.; Carburetion: 4-barrel.
Available engine: 455-4 (High Performance) V8; dual exhausts.
Transmission: Standard: 3-speed Manual (column shift mounted). Available: 3-speed Turbo Hydra-matic 400 Automatic Transmission.

Rear Axle Ratio: 3-speed Manual: 3.42; 3-speed Automatic Transmission: 2.93. Consult your Buick dealer for information on available ratios.

Centurion Comfort
Convenience. Comfort as you like it. Enjoy: Full-Flo ventilation system; heater and defroster; front door-operated interior light; glove compartment light; smoking set; rear seat ash

---

Inside Centurion
Formal luxury. Comfort. Relaxation and convenience await your pleasure in the 1971 Centurion 4-Door Hardtop Sedan.
Front head room: 38.4 inches;
Rear head room: 37.4 inches;
Front leg room: 42.6 inches;
Rear leg room: 38.5 inches;
Front shoulder room: 62.2 inches;
Rear shoulder room: 63.3 inches.

Outside Centurion
Sleek new profile. Exciting styling. Beautiful from any angle, the Centurion 4-Door Hardtop Sedan boasts the following exterior dimensions: Length: 220.7 inches; Width: 79.7 inches; Height: 53.8 inches; Wheelbase: 124.0 inches. (Note: Centurion interior and exterior dimensions are approximations in inches.)

Centurion Performance
Responsive. Dependable and reliable. Something to believe in. Yours to command.

Standard engine: 455-4 V8; Compression ratio: 8.5:1; Displacement: 455 C.I.D.; Carburetion: 4-barrel.
Available engine: 455-5 (High Performance) V8; dual exhausts.
Transmission: Standard: 3-speed Manual (column shift mounted). Available: 3-speed Turbo Hydra-matic 400 Automatic Transmission.
Rear Axle Ratio: 3-speed Manual: 3.42; 3-speed Automatic Transmission: 2.93. Consult

your Buick dealer for information on available ratios.

Centurion Comfort
Consider the comfort and convenience you would enjoy in your new automobile. Centurion has them all: Full-Flo ventilation system; heater and defroster; front door-operated interior light; glove compartment light; smoking set; rear seat ash trays; Magic-Mirror exterior finish; front and rear carpeting; arm rests; deluxe

trays; Magic-Mirror exterior finish; front and rear carpeting; arm rests; deluxe steering wheel; custom interior trims; new more convenient seat belt assembly; new full-foam seats; padded head restraints; newly designed instrument panel for easier reading and serviceability; anti-theft key warning buzzer; anti-theft steering column lock and many more comfort and convenience features your Buick dealer will be pleased to discuss with you.

Centurion Special Features
The features you would expect to find in the Buick Centurion. Enjoy: Buick's AccuDrive with forward mounted steering gear and linkage; 6,000 mile lubricated front suspension; self-adjusting power front disc brakes with composite cast iron rear drum brakes; H78 x 15 bias belted tires; direct acting hydraulic shock absorbers; Delcotron generator; Full-Flow oil filter; semi-closed cooling system; inside rear view mirror mounted on windshield; time-modulated carburetor

choke control; new evaporative emission control system; four-way hazard warning flasher; radio antenna concealed in the windshield; newly designed instrument panel for easier reading and serviceability. For additional information on other features available, please consult your Buick dealer.

Some of the equipment shown or described is available at extra cost.

---

trays; Magic-Mirror exterior finish; front and rear carpeting; arm rests; deluxe steering wheel; custom interior trims: new, more convenient seat belt assembly; new full-foam seats; padded head restraints; newly designed instrument panel for easier reading and serviceability; anti-theft key warning buzzer; anti-theft steering column lock and many more comfort and convenience features your Buick dealer will be pleased to discuss with you.

Centurion Special Features
The features you want. Centurion has them as standard equipment: Buick's Accu-Drive with forward mounted steering gear and linkage; 6,000 mile lubricated front suspension system; self-adjusting power front disc brakes with composite cast iron rear drum brakes; H78 x 15 bias belted tires; direct acting hydraulic shock absorbers; Delcotron generator; Full-Flow oil filter; semi-closed cooling system; inside rear view mirror mounted on windshield; time-modulated

carburetor choke control; new evaporative emission control system; four-way hazard warning flasher; radio antenna concealed in the windshield; newly designed instrument panel for easier reading and serviceability. For additional information on other features available, please consult your Buick dealer.

Some of the equipment shown or described is available at extra cost.

---

steering wheel; custom interior trims; new, more convenient seat belt assembly; new full-foam seats; padded head restraints; newly designed instrument panel for easier reading and serviceability; anti-theft key warning buzzer; anti-theft steering column lock and many more comfort and convenience features your Buick dealer will be pleased to discuss in detail with you.

Centurion Special Features
The features you would expect to find in the Buick Centurion. Enjoy: Buick's AccuDrive with forward mounted steering gear and linkage; 6,000 mile lubricated front suspension; self-adjusting power front disc brakes with composite cast iron rear drum brakes; H78 x 15 bias belted tires; direct acting hydraulic shock absorbers; Delcotron generator; Full-Flow oil filter; semi-closed cooling system; inside rear view mirror mounted on windshield; time-modulated carburetor

choke control; new evaporative emission control system; four-way hazard warning flasher; radio antenna concealed in the windshield; newly designed instrument panel for easier reading and serviceability. For additional information on other features available, please consult your Buick dealer.

Some of the equipment shown or described is available at extra cost.

**Centurion
Interior Seating
Appointments.**

Fabulous fabrics...durable vinyl ...rich and comfortable.
1. Elk-Grain Expanded Vinyl and Madrid-Grain Vinyl Notch Back Seats on the Centurion Hardtop Sedan and Formal Coupe are available in Green, Sandalwood, Saddle or Black.

Elk-Grain Expanded Vinyl and Madrid-Grain Vinyl Notch Back Seats are available on the Centurion Convertible in Blue, Pearl White, Saddle or Black.
2. Kipling Cloth and Madrid-Grain Vinyl Notch Back Seat is available on the Centurion Hardtop Sedan in Sandalwood or Black.

The new 1971 Centurion control center enables the driver to almost instantly operate controls and see instruments and gauges at a glance.

Some of the equipment shown or described is available at extra cost.

1972 Centurion.

Centurion Formal Coupe shown in Seamist Green with a Black vinyl top and equipped with nickel-plated engine exhaust

valves.

1972 Centurion.

Centurion 4-Door Hardtop shown in Cascade Blue with a White vinyl top.

Centurion Convertible with Customline boot cover.

1972 Centurion.

Elk-grain expanded vinyl and Madrid-grain vinyl notchback seat shown in Saddle (1).

1. Elk-grain expanded vinyl and Madrid-grain vinyl notchback seat shown in Saddle. This seat design is available in the Centurion Formal Coupe and 4-Door Hardtop in Green, Sandalwood, Saddle or Black and in the Convertible in Green, White, Saddle or Black.

2. Kenway cloth and Madrid-grain vinyl notchback seat. Available in the Centurion 4-Door Hardtop in Sandalwood or Black and in the Formal Coupe in Sandalwood.

1972 CENTURION SPECIFICATIONS.

CENTURION ENGINES, TRANSMISSIONS AND AXLE RATIOS.

Engine, standard: 455-4; Compression: 8.5:1; Displacement: 455 C.I.D.; Carburetion: 4-barrel.

Engine, available: 455-4, higher performance with dual exhaust; Displacement: 455 C.I.D.; Compression: 8.5:1; Carburetion: 4-barrel.

Transmission, standard: Turbo Hydra-matic 400 automatic.

Axle Ratio: 2.93:1. Please check your Buick dealer for available ratios.

INSIDE THE CENTURION.
(approximations in inches.)

Formal Coupe: Front head room: 38.1; Rear head room: 37.1; Front leg room: 42.6; Rear leg room: 35.5; Front shoulder room: 64.3; Rear shoulder room: 62.2.

4-Door Hardtop: Front head room: 38.4; Rear head room: 37.4; Front leg room: 42.6; Rear leg room: 38.5; Front shoulder room: 64.3; Rear shoulder room: 63.3.

Convertible: Front head room: 38.9; Rear head room: 38.1; Front leg room: 42.6; Rear leg room: 35.5; Front shoulder room: 64.3; Rear shoulder room: 61.7.

OUTSIDE THE CENTURION.
(approximations in inches.)

Formal Coupe: Length: 221.9; Width: 80.0; Height: 53.6; Wheelbase: 124.0.

4-Door Hardtop: Length: 221.9; Width: 80.0; Height: 53.8; Wheelbase: 124.0.

Convertible: Length: 221.9; Width: 80.0; Height: 53.9; Wheelbase: 124.0.

SOME SPECIAL CENTURION FEATURES.

Power front disc brakes with composite cast iron rear drum brakes, variable ratio power steering, Delcotron generator, semi-closed cooling system, time-modulated carburetor choke control, evaporative emission system, H78-15 bias belted tires, AccuDrive, an instrument panel designed for easier reading and serviceability, energy absorbing steering column, side guard beam construction and much more.

For further information on standard and available equipment and features on the above cars, see your Buick Dealer.

Centurion Hardtop Coupe.

a family car or a very personal road car, depends on whether your family is with you or not. **1973 Centurion.**

Centurion Hardtop Sedan (foreground), Centurion Convertible.

1973 Centurion.

1. Oxen-grain Expanded Vinyl and Madrid-grain Vinyl Notchback seat standard in Centurion Hardtop Coupe and Hardtop Sedan in Green, Sandalwood, Saddle or Black.

2. Manchester Cloth and Madrid-grain Vinyl 60/40 Notchback seat available in Centurion Hardtop Coupe and Hardtop Sedan in Blue or Sandalwood.

3. Manchester Cloth and Madrid-grain Vinyl Notchback seat standard in Centurion Hardtop Sedan in Blue or Sandalwood.

4. Oxen-grain Expanded Vinyl and Madrid-grain Vinyl 60/40 Notchback seat available in Green, Sandalwood, Saddle or Black. Standard in Centurion Convertible, available in Centurion Hardtop Coupe and Hardtop Sedan.

2

1973 Centurion.

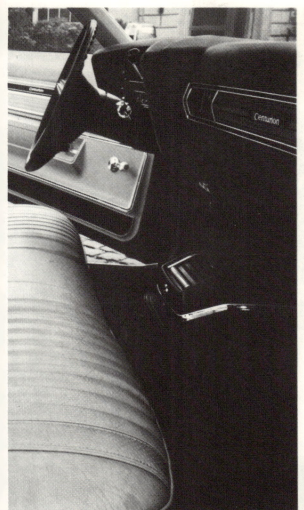

1973 Centurion specifications.

Engines, transmissions and axle ratios.

Engine, standard:
350 C.I.D. V-8.
Carburetion: 4-barrel.

Engine, available:
455 C.I.D. V-8.
Carburetion: 4-barrel.

Engine, available:
455 C.I.D. V-8.
Carburetion: modified 4-barrel with dual exhaust.

Transmission, standard:
Turbo Hydra-matic 375B automatic.

Transmission, available:
Turbo Hydra-matic 400 automatic (with 455 C.I.D. V-8 engine).

Axle Ratio: 3.08:1. Please consult your Buick dealer for information on available ratios.

Inside the Centurion. (approx. inches)

Hardtop Coupe: Front head room: 38.1; Rear head room: 37.1; Front leg room: 42.6; Rear leg room: 35.8; Front shoulder room: 64.3; Rear shoulder room: 62.2.

Hardtop Sedan: Front head room: 38.4; Rear head room: 37.4; Front leg room: 42.6; Rear leg room: 38.8; Front shoulder room: 64.3; Rear shoulder room: 63.3.

Convertible: Front head room: 38.9; Rear head room: 38.1; Front leg room: 42.6; Rear leg room: 35.8; Front shoulder room: 64.3; Rear shoulder room: 61.7.

Outside the Centurion. (approx. inches)

Hardtop Coupe: Length: 224.2; Width: 79.6; Height: 53.6; Wheelbase: 124.0.

Hardtop Sedan: Length: 224.2; Width: 79.6; Height: 53.8; Wheelbase: 124.0.

Convertible: Length: 224.2; Width: 79.6; Height: 54.2; Wheelbase: 124.0.

Some special Centurion features.

New Exhaust Gas Recirculation (EGR) and Air Injection Reactor (AIR) emission control systems, evaporative emission control system, AccuDrive, side guard beams, new computer-selected chassis springs, trued tires and concentric wheels, Full-Flo ventilation, inward-folding convertible top, carpeting front and rear, custom steering wheel, deluxe wheel covers, new larger rear window on Hardtop Coupe and many more.

For further information on features, standard and available equipment, see your Buick dealer.

3

4

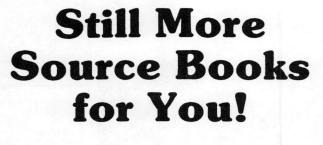